MUSCLECAR & HI-PO ENGINES
FORD
351C & BOSS 351

A book in the The Hot Rod Magazine
'Great American Engine' series.

ISBN 9781855201057

BROOKLANDS BOOKS LTD.
P.O. BOX 904, AMERSHAM,
BUCKS. HP6 9JA. UK
sales@brooklands-books.com

www.brooklandsbooks.com

ROAD TEST SERIES

Abarth Road Test Portfolio 1950-1971
AC Cars 1904-2011
AC Ace Aceca Road Test Portfolio 1953-1962
AC & Cobra 1962-2011
Alfa Romeo A Brooklands Portfolio 1920-1940
Alfa Romeo Giulietta Gold Portfolio 1954-1965
Alfa Romeo Giulia Berlina Lim. Edit. Extra 1962-1976
Alfa Romeo Giulia Coupes Lim. Edit. Ultra 1973-1976
Alfa Romeo Alfasud 1972-1984
Alfa Romeo Alfetta Gold Portfolio 1972-1987
Alfa Romeo Alfetta GTV6 1980-1986
Alfa Romeo Spider Ultimate Portfolio 1966-1994
Alfa Romeo Spider & GTV Perf. Port. 1995-2005
Allard Limited Edition Ultra
Alpine Renault Ultimate Portfolio 1958-1995
Alvis Gold Portfolio 1919-1967
AMC Rambler Limited Edition Extra 1956-1969
AMX & Javelin Gold Portfolio 1968-1974
Armstrong Siddeley Gold Portfolio 1945-1960
Aston Martin Gold Portfolio 1921-1947
Aston Martin Ultimate Portfolio 1948-1968
Aston Martin Ultimate Portfolio 1968-1980
Aston Martin Ultimate Portfolio 1981-1993
Aston Martin Ultimate Portfolio 1994-2006
Auburn Cord Duesenberg - A Brooklands Portfolio
Audi Quattro Gold Portfolio 1980-1991
Audi TT Performance Portfolio 1998-2006
Austin Seven & Ten Road Test Portfolio
Austin-Healey 100 & 100/6 Gold Port. 1952-1959
Austin-Healey 3000 Road Test Portfolio
Austin-Healey Sprite Bug-Eye Mk 1 Road Test Portfolio
Avanti Limited Edition Extra
Bentley & Rolls-Royce Portfolio 1990-2002
Berkeley Sportscars Limited Edition
BMW 700 Limited Edition 1959-1965
BMW 2002 Ultimate Portfolio 1968-1976
BMW 6 Cylinder Coupes & Saloons Gold P. 1969-1976
BMW 320, 323, 325 (6 cyl.) Gold Port. 1977-1990
BMW 3 Series Gold Portfolio 1991-1997
BMW M3 Ultimate Portfolio 1986-2006
BMW M5 Gold Portfolio 1980-2003
BMW 5 Series Gold Portfolio 1988-1995
BMW 6 Series Ultimate Portfolio 1976-1989
BMW 7 Series Performance Portfolio 1977-1986
BMW 7 Series Performance Portfolio 1986-1993
BMW 8 Series Performance Portfolio
BMW X5 Limited Edition Extra 1999-2006
BMW Alpina Performance Portfolio 1967-1987
BMW Alpina Performance Portfolio 1988-1998
BMW Z3, M Coupe & M Roadster Gold Port. 1996-02
Bond Cars 1949-1974 Road Test Portfolio
Borgward Isabella Limited Edition
Bricklin Golf Portfolio 1974-1975
Bristol Cars Portfolio
Bugatti Type 10 to Type 40 Road Test Portfolio
Bugatti Type 41 to Type 55 Road Test Portfolio
Bugatti Type 57 to Type 251 Road Test Portfolio
Bugatti Type 10 to Type 251 Road Test Portfolio
Buick Performance Portfolio 1947-1962
Buick Muscle Portfolio 1963-1973
Buick Riviera Performance Portfolio 1963-1978
Cadillac Performance Portfolio 1948-1958
Cadillac Performance Portfolio 1959-1966
Cadillac Eldorado Performance Portfolio 1967-1978
Cadillac Allante Limited Edition Extra
Caterham Seven Road Test Portfolio 1974-1999
Caterham Seven Road Test Portfolio 2000-2010
Checker Automobiles Road Test Portfolio
Impala & SS Muscle Portfolio 1958-1972
Corvair Performance Portfolio 1959-1969
Chevy II & Nova SS Gold Portfolio 1962-1974
Chevelle & SS Gold Portfolio 1964-1972
Camaro Muscle Portfolio 1967-1973
Blazer & Jimmy Limited Edition Extra 1969-1982
Blazer & Jimmy Limited Edition Extra 1983-1994
Camaro Performance Portfolio 1993-2000
Chevrolet Caprice Road Test Portfolio 1965-1990
Chevrolet Corvair Performance Portfolio 1959-1965
Chevrolet Corvette Gold Portfolio 1953-1962
Chevrolet Corvette Sting Ray Gold Port. 1963-1967
Chevrolet Corvette Gold Portfolio 1968-1977
Chrysler Imperial Gold Portfolio 1951-1975
Chrysler 300 Gold Portfolio 1955-1970
Citroen Traction Avant Limited Edition Premier
Citroen 2CV Ultimate Portfolio 1948-1990
Citroen DS & ID 1955-1975
Citroen DS & ID Gold Portfolio 1955-1975
Citroen CX Road Test Portfolio
Citroen SM Limited Edition 1970-1975
Shelby Cobra Gold Portfolio 1962-1969
Crosley & Crosley Specials Limited Edition
Cunningham Automobiles 1951-1955
Daimler SP250 Dart & V-8 2.5 litre 250 RTP 1959-69
Datsun Roadsters Performance Portfolio 1960-71
Datsun 240Z & 260Z Road Test Portfolio
Datsun 280Z & 280ZX Road Test Portfolio
Delahaye Road Test Portfolio
Delage Road Test Portfolio
DeLorean Gold Portfolio 1977-1995
De Soto Limited Edition 1952-1960
Dodge Limited Edition 1949-1959
Dodge Dart Limited Edition Extra 1960-1976
Dodge Muscle Portfolio 1964-1971
Charger Muscle Portfolio 1966-1974
Edsel Limited Edition 1957-1960
Excalibur Collection No. 1 1952-1981
Elva Sports Racers Road Test Portfolio
ERA Gold Portfolio 1934-1994
Facel Vega Limited Edition Extra 1954-1964
Ferrari Road Cars 1946-1956 Road Test Portfolio
Ferrari Dino Limited Edition Extra 1965-1974
Ferrari 308 & Mondial Ultimate Portfolio 1975-85
Ferrari 328 348 Mondial Ultimate Portfolio 1986-94
Ferrari F355 & 360 Gold Portfolio 1995-2004

www.brooklandsbooks.com

Fiat 500 1936-1972 Road Test Portfolio
Fiat 600 & 850 Gold Portfolio 1955-1972
Fiat Dino Road Test Portfolio
Fiat 124 Spider Performance Portfolio 1966-1985
Fiat Abarth 1972-1987 Road Test Portfolio
Fiat X1/9 Gold Portfolio 1973-1989
Fiat Barchetta Road Test Portfolio
Ford Zephyr, Zodiac, Executive Mk. III & IV 1962-1971
High Performance Capris Gold Portfolio 1969-1987
Capri Muscle Portfolio 1974-1987
High Performance Fiestas 1979-1991
Ford Escort RS & Mexico Limited Edition 1970-1979
Ford Thunderbird Performance Portfolio 1955-1957
Ford Thunderbird Performance Portfolio 1958-1963
Ford Thunderbird Performance Portfolio 1964-1976
Ford Fairlane Performance Portfolio 1955-1970
Ford Edsel 1957-1960 Road Test Limited Edition
Ford Ranchero Muscle Portfolio 1957-1979
Falcon Performance Portfolio 1960-1970
Ford Galaxie and LTD Gold Portfolio 1960-1976
Ford GT40 & GT Ultimate Portfolio 1964-2006
Ford Torino Performance Portfolio 1968-1974
Ford Bronco 4x4 Performance Portfolio 1966-1977
Shelby Mustang Ultimate Portfolio 1965-1970
Mustang Muscle Portfolio 1967-1973
High Performance Mustang IIs 1974-1978
Mustang 5.0L Muscle Portfolio 1982-1993
Ginetta Cars Limited Edition Ultra 1958-2007
Goggomobil Limited Edition
Hispano-Suiza Road Test Portfolio
Holden 1948-1962
Honda S500, S600, S800 Limited Edition
Honda - Acura NSX Ultimate Portfolio 1989-2005
Honda CRX 1983-1987
Hudson Performance Portfolio 1946-1957
International Scout Gold Portfolio 1961-1980
Isetta Gold Portfolio 1953-1964
ISO & Bizzarrini Limited Edition Ultra 1962-1974
Jaguar XK120, XK140, XK150 Gold Portfolio
Jaguar Mk 7, 8, 10 & 420 Road Test Portfolio
Jaguar Mk 1 & Mk 2 1955-1969 Road Test Portfolio
Jaguar E-Type Ultimate Portfolio 1961-1975
Jaguar XJ6 Series I & II Gold Portfolio 1968-1979
Jaguar XJ6 Series III Perf. Portfolio 1979-1986
Jaguar XJ-S V12 Ultimate Portfolio 1988-1996
Jaguar XK8 & XKR Performance Portfolio 1996-2005
Jeep CJ-5 Limited Edition 1960-1975
Jeep CJ-5 & CJ-7 4x4 Perf. Portfolio 1976-1986
Jeep Wagoneer Performance Portfolio 1963-1991
Jeep J-Series Pickups 1970-1982
Jeepster & Commando Limited Edition 1967-1973
Jeep Cherokee & Comanche Pickups P. P. 1984-1991
Jeep Wrangler 4x4 Performance Portfolio 1987-1999
Jeep Cherokee & Grand Cherokee 4x4 P. P. 1992-1998
Jensen Road Test Portfolio 1934-1965
Jensen Interceptor Ultimate Portfolio 1966-1992
Jensen -Healey Road Test Portfolio 1972-1976
Jowett Road Test Portfolio
Kaiser - Frazer Limited Edition 1946-1955
Lagonda Gold Portfolio 1919-1964
Lancia Aurelia & Flaminia Gold Portfolio 1950-1970
Lancia Fulvia Gold Portfolio 1963-1976
Lancia Montecarlo & Scorpion 1975-1982 RTP
Lancia Stratos Limited Edition Extra
Lancia Delta & integrale Ultimate Portfolio
Land Rover Series I, II & IIA Gold Portfolio 1948-1971
Land Rover 90 110 Defender Gold Portfolio 1983-1994
Lamborghini Performance Portfolio 1964-1976
Lamborghini Performance Portfolio 1977-1989
Lamborghini Gold Portfolio 1990-2004
Lincoln Gold Portfolio 1949-1960
Lincoln Continental Performance Portfolio 1961-1969
Lola Sports Racing Cars Limited Ed. Premier 1958-1985
Lotus Sports Racers Portfolio 1951-1965
Lotus Seven Gold Portfolio 1957-1973
Lotus Elite Limited Edition 1957-1964
Lotus Elan Ultimate Portfolio 1962-1974
Lotus Cortina Road Test Portfolio
Lotus Elite & Eclat Road Test Portfolio 1984-1972
Lotus Excel Road Test Portfolio
Lotus Europa Gold Portfolio 1966-1975
Lotus Elise & Exige Gold Portfolio 1995-2005
Marcos Coupés & Spyders Gold Portfolio 1960-1997
Maserati Cars Performance Portfolio 1957-1970
Maserati Cars Performance Portfolio 1971-1982
Maserati Cars Performance Portfolio 1982-1998
Maserati Cars Ultimate Portfolio 1999-2007
Matra Road Test Portfolio
Mazda Miata MX-5 Performance Portfolio 1989-1997
Mazda Miata MX-5 Performance Portfolio 1998-2005
McLaren F1 • GTR • LM Sportscar Perf. Portfolio
Mercedes-Benz 1925-1939 - A Portfolio
Mercedes 190SL 300SL 300SLR - A Portfolio
Mercedes S & 600 Limited Edition Extra 1965-1972
Mercedes S Class Limited Edition Extra 1980-1991
Mercedes 230SL 250SL 280SL Ultimate Port. 1963-1971
Mercedes-Benz SLs & SLCs Ultimate Port. 1971-1989
Mercedes SLs Performance Portfolio 1989-1994
Mercedes E-Class W124 Road Test Portfolio 1986-1995
Mercedes G-Wagen Gold Portfolio 1981-2005
Mercedes AMG Gold Portfolio 1983-1999
Mercedes AMG Ultimate Portfolio 2000-2006
Mercury Gold Portfolio 1947-1966
Mercury Comet & Cyclone Lim. Edit. Extra 1960-1975
Mercury Cougar Muscle Portfolio 1967-1973
Messerschmitt Gold Portfolio 1954-1964
MG Gold Portfolio 1929-1939
MG TD & TF Gold Portfolio 1949-1955
MG Y Type & Magnette Road Test Portfolio
MGA & Twin Cam Gold Portfolio 1955-1962
MG Midget Road Test Portfolio 1961-1979
MGB Roadsters 1962-1980
MGB MGC & V8 Gold Portfolio 1962-1980
MGF & TF Performance Portfolio 1995-2005
Mini Gold Portfolio 1959-1969
Mini Gold Portfolio 1969-1980
Mini Gold Portfolio 1981-1997
High Performance Minis Gold Portfolio 1960-1973
Mini Cooper Gold Portfolio 1961-1971
Mini Moke Ultimate Portfolio 1964-1994
Starion & Conquest Performance Portfolio 1982-1990
Mitsubishi 3000GT & Dodge Stealth P.P. 1990-1999
Morgan Three-Wheelers Ultimate Portfolio 1909-52
Morgan Four-Wheelers Ultimate Portfolio 1936-67
Morgan Ultimate Portfolio 1968-1990
Morgan Ultimate Portfolio 1991-2009
Morris Minor MM & Series II Road Test Portfolio
Morris Minor 1000 Road Test Portfolio
Nash Limited Edition Extra 1949-1957
Nash-Austin Metropolitan Gold Portfolio 1954-1962
Nissan 350Z Road Test Portfolio
Nissan Skyline GT-R Ultimate Portfolio 1969-2010
Noble Sports Cars Road Test Portfolio
NSU Ro80 Limited Edition
Oldsmobile 1948-1963 Limited Edition Premier
Oldsmobile Cutlass & 4-4-2 Muscle Port. 1964-1974
Oldsmobile Muscle Cars 1964-1971
Oldsmobile Toronado 1966-1978
Opel GT Ultimate Portfolio 1968-1973
Packard Automobiles 1920-1958 - A Portfolio
Pantera Ultimate Portfolio 1970-1995
Panther Gold Portfolio 1972-1990
Plymouth Limited Edition 1950-1960
Plymouth Fury Limited Edition Extra 1956-1976
Barracuda Muscle Portfolio 1964-1974
Plymouth Muscle Portfolio 1964-1971
Pontiac 1946-1963 Limited Edition Premier
High Performance Firebirds 1982-1988
Firebird & Trans Am Performance Portfolio 1993-00
Pontiac Fiero Performance Portfolio 1984-1988
Porsche Sports Racing Cars UP 1952-1968
Porsche 917 • 935 • 956 • 962 Gold Portfolio
Porsche 365 Ultimate Portfolio 1952-1965
Porsche 911 1965-1969
Porsche 911 SC & Turbo Gold Portfolio 1978-1983
Porsche 911 Ultimate Portfolio 1990-1997
Porsche 911 Ultimate Portfolio 1998-2004
Porsche 912 Limited Edition Extra 1965-1976
Porsche 914 Ultimate Portfolio
Porsche 924 Gold Portfolio 1975-1988
Porsche 928 Gold Portfolio 1977-1995
Porsche 928 Takes On The Competition
Porsche 944 Ultimate Portfolio
Porsche 968 Limited Edition Extra
Porsche Boxster Ultimate Portfolio 1996-2004
Railton & Brough Superior Gold Portfolio 1933-1950
Range Rover Gold Portfolio 1970-1985
Range Rover Gold Portfolio 1985-1995
Range Rover Performance Portfolio 1995-2001
Riley RM Series Pathfinder 2.6 A Brooklands Port.
Rolls-Royce Silver Cloud & Bentley S Ultimate Port.
Rolls-Royce Silver Shadow Ultimate Port. 1965-80
Rover P4 1949-1959
Rover P6 1963-1977
Rover 2000 & 2200 1963-1977
Saab Sonett Collection No. 1 1966-1974
Studebaker Ultimate Portfolio 1946-1966
Studebaker Hawks & Larks Limited Edit. Premier 1956-66
Avanti Limited Edition Extra 1962-1991
Subaru Impreza WRX Performance Port. 2001-2005
Sunbeam Alpine Limited Edition Extra 1959-1968
Sunbeam Tiger Limited Edition Extra 1964-1967
Suzuki SJ Gold Portfolio 1971-1997
Tatra Cars Road Test Portfolio
Toyota Land Cruiser Gold Portfolio 1956-1987
Toyota Land Cruiser 1988-1997
Toyota Supra Performance Portfolio 1982-1998
Toyota MR2 Road Test Portfolio 1984-1989
Toyota MR2 Road Test Portfolio 1990-1999
Toyota MR2 Road Test Portfolio 2000-2007
Triumph TR2 & TR3 Road Test Portfolio
Triumph TR4, TR5 & TR250 Road Test Portfolio
Triumph TR6 Road Test Portfolio
Triumph Herald 1959-1971
Triumph Vitesse 1962-1971
Triumph 2000, 2.5, 2500 1963-1977
Triumph GT6 Gold Portfolio 1966-1974
Triumph Spitfire Road Test Portfolio
Triumph Stag Road Test Portfolio
TVR Limited Edition Ultra 1958-1985
TVR Performance Portfolio 1986-1994
TVR Performance Portfolio 2000-2005
VW Beetle Gold Portfolio 1935-1967
VW Beetle Gold Portfolio 1968-1991
VW Bus Camper Van Perf. Portfolio 1954-1967
VW Bus Camper Van Perf. Portfolio 1968-1979
VW Bus Camper Van Perf. Portfolio 1979-1991
VW Karmann Ghia Gold Portfolio 1955-1974
VW Golf GTI Limited Edition Extra 1976-1991
VW Golf Cabriolet 1979-2002 Road Test Portfolio
VW Corrado Limited Edition Premier 1989-1995
Volvo PV444 & PV544 Perf. Portfolio 1945-1965
Volvo 120 Amazon Ultimate Portfolio
Volvo 1800 Ultimate Portfolio 1960-1973
Volvo 140 & 160 Series Gold Portfolio 1966-1975
Westfield Performance Portfolio 1982-2004

MILITARY VEHICLES

Complete WW2 Military Jeep Manual
Dodge WW2 Military Portfolio 1940-1945
German Military Equipment WW2
Hail To The Jeep
Combat Land Rover Portfolio No. 1
Land Rover Military Portfolio
Off Road Jeeps Civilian & Military 1944-1971
US Military Vehicles 1941-1945
Standard Military Motor Vehicles-TM9-2800 (WW2)
VW Kubelwagen Military Portfolio 1940-1990
WW2 Allied Vehicles Military Portfolio 1939-1945
WW2 Jeep Military Portfolio 1941-1945

RACING & THE LAND SPEED RECORD

The Land Speed Record 1898-1919
The Land Speed Record 1920-1929
The Land Speed Record 1930-1939
The Land Speed Record 1940-1962
The Land Speed Record 1963-1999
Can-Am Racing 1966-1969
Can-Am Racing 1970-1974
The Carrera Panamericana Mexico - 1950-1954
Le Mans - The Bentley & Alfa Years - 1923-1939
Le Mans - The Jaguar Years - 1949-1957
Le Mans - The Ferrari Years - 1958-1965
Le Mans - The Ford & Matra Years - 1966-1974
Le Mans - The Porsche Years - 1975-1982
Le Mans - The Porsche & Jaguar Years - 1983-91
Le Mans - The Porsche & Peugeot Years - 1992-99
Mille Miglia - The Alfa & Ferrari Years - 1927-1951
Mille Miglia - The Ferrari & Mercedes Years - 1952-57
Targa Florio - The Porsche & Ferrari Years - 1955-64
Targa Florio - The Porsche Years - 1965-1973
Brabham Ralt Honda The Ron Tauranac

RESTORATION & GUIDE SERIES

BMW 2002 - A Comprehensive Guide
BMW 02 Restoration Guide
BMW E30 - 3 Series Restoration Bible
BMW E36 - 3 Series Restoration Tips & Techniques
BMW - 5 & 6 Series Restoration Tips & Techniques
Classic Camaro Restoration
Engine Swapping Tips & Techniques
Ferrari Life Buyer's Portfolio
Land Rover Restoration Portfolio
PC on Land Rover Series I Restoration
Lotus Elan Restoration Guide
Lotus Twin Cam Engines
MG T Series Restoration Guide
MGA Restoration Guide
PC on MGB Restoration
Mustang Restoration Tips & Techniques
Practical Gas Flow
Range Rover - The First Fifty
Restoring Sprites & Midgets an Enthusiast's Guide
Solex Carburettors Tuning Tips and Techniques
SU Carburetters Tuning Tips & Techniques
The Great Classic Muscle Cars Compared
Weber Carburettors Tuning Tips and Techniques

ROAD & TRACK SERIES

Road & Track on Aston Martin 1962-1990
Road & Track on Austin Healey 1953-1970
R & T BMW Z3, M Coupe & M Roadster Port. 96-02
R & T Camaro & Firebird Portfolio 1993-2002
Road & Track Dodge Viper Portfolio 1992-2002
Road & Track Ferrari V-12 Portfolio 1992-2002
Road & Track Ferrari F355 360 F430 Portfolio 95-06
R & T Jaguar XJ-S - XK8 - XKR Portfolio 1975-2003
Road & Track MX-5 Miata Portfolio 1989-2002
R & T Mercedes SL - SLK - CLK Portfolio 1990-2003
Road & Track on MG Sports Cars 1949-1961
Road & Track on MG Sports Cars 1962-1980
Road & Track Mustang Portfolio 1994-2002
Road & Track Nissan 300ZX & 350Z Portfolio 1984-03
Road & Track Porsche 928 Portfolio 1977-1994
Road & Track Porsche 911 Portfolio 1990-1997
Road & Track - Peter Egan Side Glances 1983-1992
Road & Track - Peter Egan Side Glances 1992-1997
Road & Track - Peter Egan Side Glances 1998-2002
Road & Track - Peter Egan Side Glances 2002-2006

HOT ROD 'ENGINE' SERIES

Chevy 265 & 283
Chevy 302 & 327
Chevy 348 & 409
Chevy 396 & 427
Chevy 454 thru 512
Chevy Monster Big Blocks
Chrysler Hemi
Chrysler 273, 318, 340 & 360
Chrysler 361, 383, 400, 413, 426 & 440
Ford 289, 302, Boss 302 & 351W
Ford 351C & Boss 351
Ford Small Block
Ford Big Block

MOTORCYCLES

To see our range of over 70 titles visit www.brooklands-books.com

CONTENTS

INTRODUCTION

Hot Rod Magazine has from its inception in January '48 been performance orientated. The key to high performance is the engine, and Hot Rod's editors have for over forty years kept their reader' interest by commissioning articles on how to maintain, tune, repair, restore and modify the popular power plants of the period.

If ever there was a golden age for the American engines it must be from mid 50's when the small block Chevy made its debut to the early 70's when emission controls brought an end to the musclecar era. The three major manufactures GM, Ford and Chrysler each supported at least one big block and one small block engine during this period which subsequently went on to become automotive legends.

This book is one of our Hot Rod on Great American series. Its purpose is to bring together a comprehensive selection of the best and most informative stories on one or one family of engines. It is targeted at todays young enthusiasts with a view to letting them know what was written about their power units during this exciting period. If older readers enjoy a nostalgic trip through these pages, so be it.

The stories included here have been drawn from Hot Rod and Car Craft magazines and from other Petersen publications of the period. We are, as always, indebted to the Petersen Publishing Company for allowing us to re-issue these copyright technical articles in this way. Our thanks also go to Lee Kelley and John Dianna for their personal help and support over the years.

R.M. Clarke

Ford · Mercury "Cleveland" V-8

351 Cubic Inches
250 and 300 Horsepower

1

The completely new Cleveland engines come both as a duplicate 250-hp 2-bbl. and as a higher-performance 300-hp 4-bbl. This last replaces last year's 290-hp 351 small-block. The new engines get their name from the place of their origin, the Cleveland Engine Plant No. 2; the older 351 is called the "Windsor" for the same reason. The Cleveland engine is definitely Ford's small V-8 of the next 5 or so years. While the bore diameter and center-to-center spacing are the same in both the 351W and 351C engine blocks, the C has a lower deck. The C block is also slightly longer than the W, as the front portion has been extended about 2 inches to envelop the timing chain and gears. This allows a flat stamping to be used to cover the timing gears, rather than needing a complicated (and therefore expensive) casting. While the present bearing caps are still held by 2 bolts, there is enough room to switch to the 4-bolt caps used in many high-performance engines. The main bearings are slightly smaller in diameter and length than those in the 351W, and the connecting rods are a couple of tenths shorter. The major difference in the 351C and 351W, however, is that the Cleve-

land engine uses canted valves, rather than having the valve stems parallel. This allows a better intake port design, and allows large-headed valves to open away from each other in the cylinder. The Cleveland heads cannot be used on the Windsor or other small-block engines, as the water passages from the block to the heads have been completely redesigned and will not mate.

GENERAL / The Cleveland engine is a cast iron 90° V-8, with pushrod-operated overhead valves. Ford numbers its cylinders starting with the front of the right bank 1-2-3-4, then 5-6-7-8 on the left bank. Firing order for the Cleveland is 1-3-7-2-6-5-4-8. Engine identification is the same as with the other Ford-Mercury engines. If there is a metal tag under the coil or on the front of the block, the year and displacement of the engine can be found. The first number group on the top line of the tag is the displacement, and the middle group is the last 2 digits of the model year. If the tag is missing, there may be a number at the front of the block such as 0J121628, wherein the 1st digit is the model year. Another number sometimes

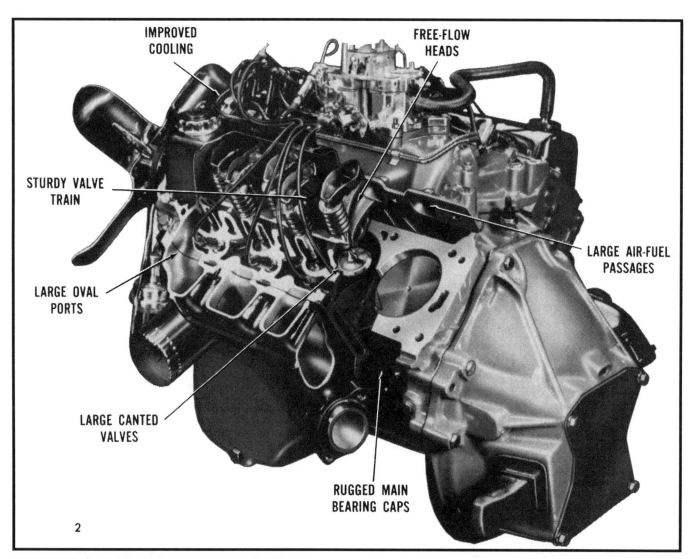

IMPROVED COOLING

FREE-FLOW HEADS

STURDY VALVE TRAIN

LARGE AIR-FUEL PASSAGES

LARGE OVAL PORTS

LARGE CANTED VALVES

RUGGED MAIN BEARING CAPS

2

4

3

1. Taking the place of the "Windsor"—the older 351-inch, 290-hp small-block—is Ford's new Cleveland V-8.

2. The Cleveland V-8—featuring wild port area—is being used in '70 Mustangs, Cougars, Torinos and Montegos.

3. The Cleveland V-8 is different from the other small-block Fords because of its block/head combination which discourages any parts swapping. Note water hole on upper portion of block—coolant does not flow through intake.

4. Oil is circulated throughout the 351C by means of a rotary mechanical pump—50-70 psi (250/351), 45-65 (300/351).

found on the front of the block in various locations is the Engine Build Date Code, such as 9J13S, wherein the 1st digit is the calendar year the engine was built and the letter next to it is the month, with "A" for January, etc., excluding "I." In the absence of any tag or stamped numbers, engines can be identified by writing down manifold casting numbers, carburetor or distributor part numbers, etc., and consulting your local Ford or Mercury dealer parts man, who can then identify the engine for you.

PISTONS / The Cleveland engine pistons are of different dimensions and weight from the Windsor engine, but are very similar in overall design. They are tin-plated autothermic alloy aluminum, with steel struts for additional strength, are cam- or elliptical-ground, and have slipper skirts. The upper compression rings are barrel-faced cast iron, with a molybdenum-filled groove, the same as in the 351W engine. The lower compression rings are tapered-face cast iron, with a scraper groove. The 351C lower rings are phosphate-coated, whereas those in the Windsor engine are oxide-coated. Oil rings are multi-piece, with 2 black-oxide-coated and chrome-plated SAE 1070 steel rails separated by an SAE 30201 rustless steel spacer-expander. Piston pins are heat-treated SAE 5015 steel (SAE 1019 optional) and are press-fitted into the forged SAE 1041-H steel connecting rod small-ends. Con rod big-end bearings are removable, steel-backed, plated copper-lead alloy.

CRANKSHAFT / As neither of the Cleveland engines is designed for extremely high performance at this time, precision-molded cast nodular iron is used for the crankshafts. The main bearing journals are slightly shorter and

Ford · Mercury "Cleveland" V-8

smaller in diameter than those of the 351W engine, so cranks are not interchangeable. The crankpin journal diameter is the same, however. The Cleveland crankshaft runs in 5 removable, steel-backed, unplated copper-lead alloy bearings, with the end-thrust taken by the center #3 bearing. A tuned, elastic-suspended, inertia member vibration damper is pressed onto the front end of the crankshaft, and is held by a bolt and washer.

CAMSHAFT / The camshaft in the Cleveland engines is in its normal place for a V-8, directly above the crankshaft at the center of the vee. It is precision-molded special alloy cast iron, and is induction-hardened and phosphate-coated. The cam runs in 5 removable steel-backed SAE 15 lead-base babbitt bearings in the block, driven by a 48-link chain connecting the sintered iron (steel optional) crankshaft sprocket to the die-cast aluminum camshaft sprocket with its nylon teeth. Cam timing for the 2-bbl. 351 Cleveland is very similar to the 2-bbl. 351 Windsor, but is not identical. The cam for the 4-bbl. 351 Cleveland has a longer valve opening duration and a bit more overlap of this opening.

VALVES / Intake valves for the Cleveland engines are #1 Silchrome steel with aluminized heads; exhaust valves are 21-4N nitrogen-treated, manganese-chromium-nickel

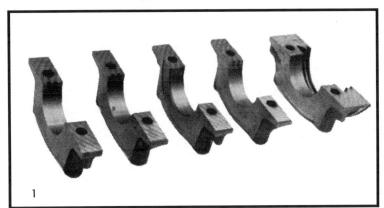

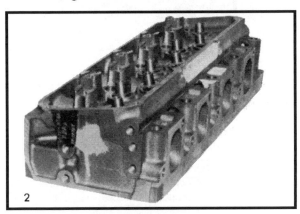

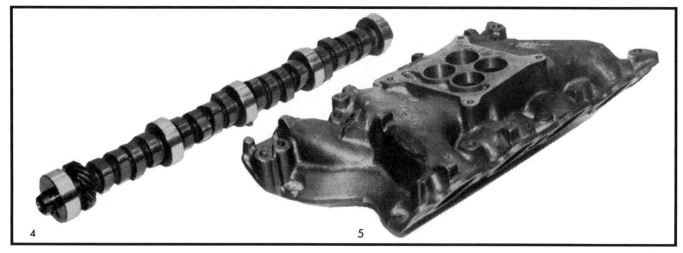

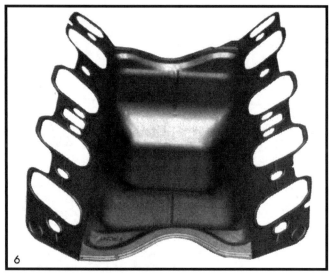

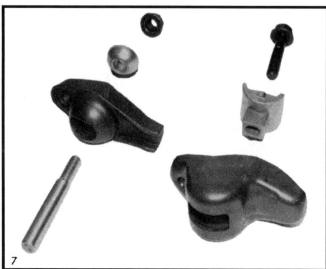

austenitic steel with aluminized heads, and with chrome-plated stems and tips for the 4-bbl. 351C. All use dampers inside the outer valve springs. Hydraulic lifters are used.

LUBRICATION / In both Cleveland engines the main bearings, connecting rod big-end bearings, camshaft bearings and hydraulic valve lifters are lubricated by oil through the galleries. The piston pins are lubricated by a timed pressure stream, the timing gears and chain by a metered pressure stream, and the cylinder walls by oil

1. Main caps house slightly smaller bearings than on 351W.

2. The main difference on the Cleveland engine are the heads with their canted valving which allows better port angle. Torquing sequence is normal (working slowly out from the center) with a maximum of 95-100 ft.-lb.

3. Still a relatively mild engine, the cranks are not forgings, but instead are precision-molded cast nodular iron. The main journals are slightly changed from the Windsor so the cranks too cannot be easily swapped.

4. Nothing wild here although the Cleveland cam features a bit more duration and overlap than the Windsor 351.

5. Low-rise intake manifold takes Autolite 4-barrel carb.

6. Note size of intake ports on this 1-piece intake gasket.

7. Rocker arms also differ. Ford's standard unit (left) bears no resemblance to the larger Cleveland rocker.

mist and crankshaft splashing. A rotary mechanical oil pump works at 50-70 psi in the 250/351C and at 45-65 psi in the 300/351C, drawing oil through a stationary shrouded screen in the crankcase, and sending it through a throwaway full-flow filter. FoMoCo recommends SAE 20W-40 for above-freezing temperatures, or SAE 30 for from freezing to 90° F and SAE 40 for above 90°.

FUEL SYSTEM / A mechanical fuel pump on the left side of the engine block works at 4.5-5.5 psi, with a permanent saran plastic filter in the gas tank, and a nylon and monel cloth filter in the gas line at the carburetor inlet. Both the 2-bbl. and the 4-bbl. carburetors for the Cleveland engines are by Autolite.

FORD-MERCURY	250/351C	300/351C
CLEVELAND V-8	V-8	V-8
Displacement (cu. in.)	351	351
Horsepower @ rpm	250 @ 4600	300 @ 5400
Horsepower per cu. in.	.710	.855
Torque (lb.-ft.) @ rpm	355 @ 2600	380 @ 3400
Bore	4.002	4.002
Stroke	3.50	3.50
Compression Ratio	9.5:1	11.0:1
Carburetion	2-bbl.	4-bbl.
1970 Engine Code	See General	See General
Length/Width/Height (in.)	28/21/22	28/21/22

It sounded like a good idea, but even to the most optimistic of observers it seems to have gotten off to a very slow start. The idea, take a Detroit compact, drop in a small-block drag motor, strip the whole thing down to 2450 pounds and then go out heads-up Pro Stock racing with the likes of Ronnie Sox, Dick Landy and Bill Jenkins. It strains the imagination to picture the amount of testing and development necessary to make such an undertaking successful. Nevertheless, under present NHRA and AHRA rules, for example, a 103-inch wheelbase (100-inch minimum) Maverick weighing 2450 lbs. (the class minimum) powered by a 350 cubic inch engine (7 lbs./cubic inch mini-

data gathered during the testing is available and worth examining.

Initially, Ford began testing with a blueprinted and slightly modified Boss 351 Ford. The testing was aimed mainly at the new 366 (6 liter) limit on the NASCAR circuit (which otherwise has absolutely no bearing on drag racing), but all the data gathered proved helpful to the drag engine builders. The engine consisted of a stock Boss block, crank and rods (short block assembly #D1ZZ-6009-D or late bare block #D1ZZ-6010-D, rod #D1ZZ-6200-A, and crank-#D1ZZ-6303-A). The stock Boss forged aluminum pistons (part #D1ZZ-6100-A or B or C, depending upon the bore dimension) had an additional .085-in. cut from the valve pock-

ets to provide the required valve-to-piston clearance necessary with the experimental NASCAR 366 cam which was installed in the engine. With this cut the total valve-to-piston clearance was measured at .120-in. The cam itself, soon to be released as a production item by Ford, provided .355-in. of intake lift at the cam (.600 at the valve) with 326° of duration. On the exhaust side .326-in. of lift (.620 at the valve) was provided with 334° of duration. The cam was initially installed 2° retarded (intake opens 18° BTDC @ .100-in. of cam lift).

The heads were Boss items (#D1ZZ-6049-A) that had been reworked in the Falconer Dunn shop in Culver City, Calif. The heads were

THE BOSS 366

Two Ford Small-Blocks for Pro Stock

ABOVE — First appearance of Terry's 366 Ford-powered Maverick Pro Stock at Gatornationals.

mum) would be legal. Though such a car is possible, to date only a single major appearance has been made by one of these mini-Pro Stockers. The then-factory-supported teams of Dick Loehr and Ed Terry showed up at the NHRA Gatornationals in Gainsville, Florida, with two Mavericks sporting Boss 351 engines.

Obviously, considerable money and effort had been expended by their backer to test the feasibility of the whole idea. First-outing bugs plagued both cars and neither was able to qualify as they could only get the cars into the low 10-second bracket. Apparently discouraged by the showing at Gainsville, it was announced shortly thereafter that Ford had withdrawn their support from the Ford Drag Teams and thus ended completely their active involvement in organized drag racing, though rumors persist that Ed Terry may still be getting some factory bucks from an "unknown" source. The future of the small-block Pro Stock seems quite uncertain but at this point some of the technical

9

milled .040 inch to give an 11:1 compression ratio. 2.190-inch titanium intake valves were installed along with 1.710-inch hollow stem exhaust valves that had been cut down to 1.675 inches. The exhaust valves were not sodium filled. The use of this valve setup eliminated any valve clash that might arise with the NASCAR 366 cam. Boss 302 Trans-Am springs and retainers were installed to complete the valve train. Total advance was set at 42° and a tunnel ram manifold was installed with dual 600-cfm Holleys. This engine produced a maximum horsepower reading of 536 @ 7000 rpm on the dyno during an extensive testing session at the Autolite dyno in Long Beach, California. This was basi-

cally the engine used in Dick Loehr's car at Gainsville.

At the same time that this testing was going on, Ed Terry and his wrench John Healy were collaborating with "Hank the Crank" Bechtloff, now operating out of his new "Hank the Crank, Inc." shop in North Hollywood, to create a stroked Boss-351 to be used in a 2565-pound Maverick. In the March issue of *Car Craft* we published a chart delineating the various bore and stroke combinations available from Hank for the 351 Ford ("Hank the Crank" Betters Ford's Ideas, *Car Craft*, March, 1971). By using these various combinations, about any desired displacement from 342 inches to 383 inches can be obtained. By utilizing a

.020-inch overbore and increasing the stroke by .100-inch, the chart tells us, a displacement of 365.51 cubic inches is realized, a size suitable for either NASCAR or drag racing (our main concern).

To begin with, a Boss 351-C 4-bolt main block was selected. The block was normally prepped for racing except that it was overbored .020-inches. During the boring process a torquing plate was fastened to the head surface of the block under normal head bolt torquing stresses so the block would be drawn into its final configuration before boring and honing. As the heads on any engine are torqued down, the block will have a tendency to twist and change configuration slightly with the

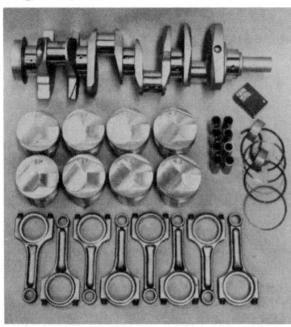

366 innards included "Hank" stroker crank, JE forged pistons, Federal Mogul bearings, Sealed Power rings, lightweight pins.

Lubrication was a problem. Pickup is in bottom of rear-mounted and deepened sump. Windage tray and connecting line to pump were added.

ABOVE — Boss 351 Heads prepared by Air Flow Research. 2.190-in. intake, 1.170 exhaust valves.

Torquing plate on Boss 4-bolt gives true cylinder alignment during .020 overbore.

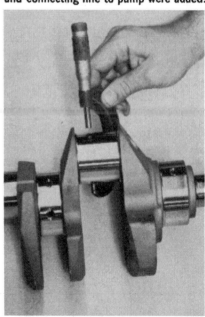

Boss crank was offset reground by "Hank the Crank" increasing stroke by .100 in.

additional support/stress exerted by the head bolts. The torquing plate simulates these pressures but allows the block to be rebored and honed into a configuration duplicating the one under which it will be running. Incidently, these plates are currently available from Hank for the 351 block. Additional valve clearance was also provided by notching the tops of each cylinder.

Next a "Hank" offset reground high nodular cast Boss crank was fitted to

Cloyes double roller chain and sprockets eliminate timing variation. Lower sprocket has three keyways, straight up, 2° advance and 2° retard to ease cam timing.

.100-inch long chrome moly "Hank the Crank" designed rods are .100 inch longer than stock, utilizes 7/16" capscrews.

Weiand small plenum top with Offenhauser bottom, dual 660 Holleys proved the best all-around intake combination.

the block. Each rod throw on the crank was reduced from 2.312 inches to 2.100 inches, reducing bearing speed and its resulting friction. At the same time the centerline of the throw was moved away from the centerline of the crank .050-in. By moving the centerline .050 the piston will move .050-in. higher in the bore and drop .050-in. lower as the crank rotates, thus the total stroke increase is .100-in. This is an extremely difficult grinding process but the end result is worth the effort. Care is taken to leave a large radius between the throw and the face of the counterweight cheek to give strength in this area. Although the effective diameter of the throw is reduced, to date there have been no failures in this area of the crank.

Specially-prepared "Hank" rods were fitted next. These chrome moly E4340 steel rods are .100-in. longer than stock giving an overall center-to-center length of 5.875-inches. Although this does not effect the displacement of the engine, it does give a much more desirable L/R ratio, thus decreasing side loading on the piston. High-strength 7/16" capscrews are also utilized along with rod bolt alignment sleeves to reduce side loads on the bolts thus increasing their life expectancy.

Hank designed pistons of forged aluminum were then selected. These pistons are 40 grams lighter than stock and were installed to a deck height of .003-inches. Sealed Power rings were fitted to the pistons. A 1/16-inch top compression ring is used along with a 1/16-inch cast second ring and a 1/8-inch medium tension (16 lbs.) oil ring. Tapered bore lightweight pins are used, fitted with double spirolocs. Federal Mogul bearings were installed with .003-inch clearance.

Air Flow Research-prepped Boss 351 heads were added next. These heads were fitted with the titanium 2.190-inch intake and the 1.710-inch hollow stem lightweight valves. Normal polishing and testing was carried out by Air Flow until maximum flow was achieved. The heads were milled from 72cc per chamber to 56cc, taking off .005-inches for the removal of each cc. Final compression ratio was 12.5:1 though some tests were made with heads of higher compression. Crane Engineering roller rockers designed for the 396/427 Chevy were used initially. These rockers proved to be too long and gave undesirable geometry. Crane Engineering has been working on a roller rocker designed specifically for the Boss 351. They are now available (#27750) and should solve this problem. Ford 302 Trans-Am (competition — only, triple only) springs (number

D0ZX-6A511-A) were used with a seat pressure of 130 pounds closed and 420 pounds open. Ford pushrods #D00Z-6565-F were used along with lifter #D1ZZ-6500-B.

Finally, some problems were encountered with the head gaskets on these engines. To eliminate these problems the racing blocks were fitted with O-rings, however, on anything but an all-out engine the Reinz-manufactured Boss .047-inch thick (compressed) gasket (black) will suffice (#D1ZZ-6051-C).

A Crane camshaft #F-276-3677-4 with a .636-inch lift and 330° duration was used for all testing. And the newly released Cloyes double roller chain and sprockets (part #9-3121) is the latest tip for valve train drive. This setup eliminates chain-stretch which had previously been quite a problem.

Induction was handled by a manifold mutation consisting of an Offenhauser Tunnel Ram bottom piece with a Weiand High Ram plenum fastened to the top. Dual 720 Holleys were used during dyno testing of the engine but dual Holley 660's proved the best setup at the track. Ignition was handled by a specially built unit from Rotofaze Ignition, designed by George Illinski. The distributor features a tall drive shaft intended to clear a Ford torque box and dual Autolite in-line carbs which were eventually to be run on the car. This setup was never run, however, as Ford withdrew before testing advanced this far.

Lubrication proved to be quite a problem when the Boss-351 was fitted into the Maverick body. The sump had to be relocated to the rear of the block and a special pickup and transfer line were built to fit to the stock oil pump. A Chrysler 392 oil spring was used in the pump to increase oil pressure and a special tunnel was built into the deepened pan to clear steering. An oil baffle was also used. Because of clearance problems with the Hooker Headers (time limitations would not allow for relocating routing and fittings) the oil filter was remote-mounted. This also served a secondary purpose of allowing additional oil cooling.

This particular engine turned in a high horsepower reading of 585 at 7200 rpm on the test dyno. All those concerned with the engine felt that it was producing enough horsepower to match the Pro-Stock standards of today and Ed Terry was able to turn a reported 9.83 at 138.96 at Fremont, California, with his car after the bugs with the suspension and chassis had finally been eliminated. But the future of this type car seems very uncertain now that acknowledged factory support has been dropped. ⊚

WHAT FORD WILL DO IN '72

If you think that Detroit's detuning dictum
tossed the Boss for a loss, just look at the Cobra
that Ford has in its snake basket.

BY FRED FREEL

Nineteen seventy-two will be just one step closer to a "clean air" environment. Compression ratios tumbled in 1970 for the first time since quality high octane gasoline was introduced, but it's still not clear as to whether the unleaded fuel route is the right one to take. At first it seemed as though Ford was going to stand pat with their high compression performance engines, but it turns out that they just needed a little more time to prepare "new" engines. And from all indications, they made the right choice. Performance did go down in 1970, and most of the regression can be blamed on the lower compression ratios needed to run on unleaded fuel. Yet, there's a chance that Ford has a couple of wild cards up their sleeve for '72, as they are doing a

little shuffling of their standard engine lineup.

The 1972 Boss will, more or less, be technically identical to this year's Mustang muscle engine, except for a decrease in compression to 8.8:1. How much this will affect power output of this relatively strong engine, we don't know. But you can expect from 10 to 20 fewer horses available at the wheels. The change to a larger combustion chamber was comparatively easy at the factory level, since all that was necessary was to cast the wide-open chamber from the 2V Cleveland head into that of the Boss. The new chamber is really open, too, and the spark plug boss reaches well into the chamber to give good flame travel.

To get the required volume for an 8.8:1 compression ratio, it was neces-

sary to switch to a flat-top forged piston. Only one eyebrow is used for valve relief, and that's on the intake side. The only other change, other than regular production updating, will be to increase the flow capacity of the 4300-D Motorcraft carburetor

1. Appearance of '72 Boss 351 will be not much different from the '71 model. Inside, it's another story.

2. The original high compression Cleveland combustion chamber was a decided "wedge," but both CJ and Boss will switch to a full open type, which was first used in 2V heads. The new heads (right) have special induction hardened valve seats to prevent wear with unleaded fuels.

3. Since the CJ will employ a new high-lift hydraulic camshaft, a new oil deflector (arrows) was designed to increase oil flow to the rocker arm fulcrums. The Boss will employ the same tried and true setup originally applied to the Boss 302.

4. Since both the Boss 351 and the new 351 CJ will employ lower compression ratios, they both needed new flat-top pistons. The Boss has a slightly higher ratio with its forged pistons, since only one "eyebrow" is used for valve clearance. The CJ will employ two eyebrows in its cast aluminum pistons.

5. There is a bit of difference in connecting rods used for both engines. The CJ unit, pictured here with cast flat-top piston, has hefty big end and a strong shank, but the Boss uses the same rods after they have been shot-peened and magnafluxed; high tensile bolts are used along with premium copper-lead bearings.

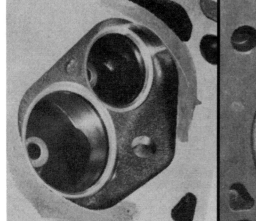
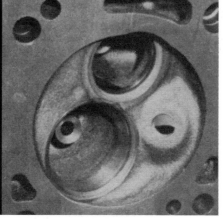

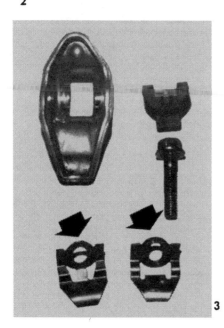

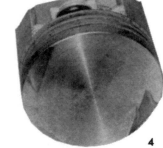

from 750 to 800 cfm.

The real news at Ford for '72 will be the 351 Cobra Jet. You are undoubtedly familiar with Ford's "middle of the road" engine tune. It's been used on both the anchor 428 and the newer 429, and is *the* hot setup with a factory hydraulic cam. The Cobra Jet (or CJ) is by no means a racing engine like the Boss is intended to be. It's more or less a crossbreeding of the advantages of the Boss and the less costly, and more docile 351 4V. From all indications the plain 4V engine will eventually be discontinued, and the CJ will be left to handle all 4-barrel applications in the Mustang and Torino (and even the Maverick!?).

What makes the CJ so different as to term it a new engine? Lend an ear . . .

A NEW COBRA JET?

From the inside out, the CJ has taken advantage of just about every Boss component that is useful in an engine designed to rev to around 6000 rpm. The object, of course, was to keep the price down, and although Ford hasn't announced the optional tag, we guesstimate that it will be only slightly higher than that of the plain 351 4V. The components borrowed from the Boss and Ford parts shelves lead us to believe that the CJ is in reality a Muscle Parts engine—built to order! All the good parts are there, except for the Boss valve train, which is only needed with mechanical valve lifters. The CJ, too, has a lowered compression ratio of 8.6:1. The reason the CJ has a slightly lower ratio than the Boss, even though they both use the same chamber shape, is because the CJ's cast pistons employ two eyebrows for valve clearance. Thus, there is more chamber volume because of the extra eyebrow. The CJ also uses a .035-in. deck-to-piston top tolerance, while the Boss can get by with as little as .013-in.

Since the reason for going to the lower compression ratio was to make possible the use of unleaded fuel, the exhaust valve seats in the cylinder head are specially induction hardened to give better durability with high valve spring pressures (the Boss has this feature, too). In the past, engineers counted on the lead content of gasoline to provide a thin lead coating on the valve seat, which acted as an anti-wear lubricant. This trick isn't applicable now, so you will probably see a number of different techniques used in the next few years to lick the valve seat wear problem.

THE RE-TUNED 4V

Putting larger combustion chambers in the standard 4V would undoubtedly inhibit performance, so Ford retuned the engine, instead of detuning as has been the practice at General Motors. In other words, the low compression CJ is expected to outperform the 1971 4V, which has the higher 10.7:1 compression ratio. Just how this is done lies mostly in the new CJ valve train and camshaft, and the addition of a larger carburetor (see comparison chart).

The standard 4V intake and exhaust valves are used in the CJ, but they are held closed by new stiffer valve springs. They aren't as tough as the Boss type, but they will give enough tension to keep things sorted out with a hydraulic cam. The cam itself is only slightly wilder in timing event than the 4V, but the overall valve lift is increased .054-in. on intake and .037-in. on exhaust. This should give pretty healthy breathing at the engine's red-line of 6000 rpm.

Although no power ratings have yet been released on either the Boss or CJ, we're just guesstimating that they will be 290 and 310 bhp, respectively. The Boss is advertised as 330 net horsepower for 1971, so there's no telling what they will announce for the new engines. Insurance companies and the smog situation have put so much pressure on future engine designs that we wouldn't be surprised to see the new CJ rated at 250 bhp. New model introductions should bare the facts.

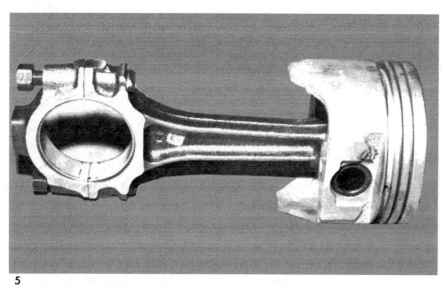

5

CLEVELAND SPECIFICATION COMPARISON

	1971		1972	
SPECIFICATIONS	351 4V	Boss 351	351 4V	Boss 351
Horsepower @ rpm	285 @ 5400	330 @ 5400	290 @ 5400*	310 @ 5400*
Torque @ rpm	370 @ 3400	370 @ 4000	360 @ 3600*	360 @ 4000*
Compression ratio	10.7:1	11.7:1	8.6:1	8.8:1
Combustion chamber volume	64.3cc	61.3cc	77.7cc*	74.7cc*
Valves	Standard	Stainless	Standard	Stainless
Valve diameter: intake	2.195 ins.	2.195 ins.	2.195 ins.	2.195 ins.
exhaust	1.715 ins.	1.715 ins.	1.715 ins.	1.715 ins.
Valve spring load (Open)	265 lbs.	315 lbs.	285 lbs.	315 lbs.
Valve lifters	Hydraulic	Mechanical	Hydraulic	Mechanical
Valve lift: intake	.427-in.	.491-in.	.481-in.	.491-in.
exhaust	.453 in.	.491-in.	.490-in.	.491-in.
Rocker arm attachment	Bolt-on arm	Thread-in stud	Bolt-on arm	Thread-in stud
Camshaft timing:				
Intake opens BTC	18°	50°	18°	50°
Intake closes ABC	70°	94°	72°	94°
Intake duration	268°	324°	270°	324°
Exhaust opens BBC	81°	102°	82°	102°
Exhaust closes ATC	19°	42°	28°	42°
Exhaust duration	280°	324°	290°	324°
Overlap	37°	92°	46°	92°
Crankshaft material	Cast Iron	Cast Iron	Cast Iron	Cast Iron
Bearing material	Babbitt	Copper-lead	Babbitt	Copper-lead
Connecting rods	Standard	Peened & fluxed	Standard	Peened & fluxed
Cylinder block type	2-bolt mains	4-bolt mains	4-bolt mains	4-bolt mains
Piston material	Cast Aluminum	Forged Aluminum	Cast Aluminum	Forged Aluminum
Carburetion	600 cfm (Ford)	750 cfm (Ford)	800 cfm (Ford)	800 cfm (Ford)
Intake manifold	Cast Iron	Cast Aluminum	Cast Iron	Cast Iron
Engine weight	620 lbs.	584 lbs.	615 lbs.	615 lbs.
*Estimated				

Manley makes the adjustable rockers, cam grinders make the solid-lifter-type sticks, and together they add up to...

RPM✚ FOR 351 FORDS

BELOW — The first step in installing the Manley adjustable rockers is to drill out the existing 5/16-inch holes with a 3/8-inch bit. Check the stock hole depth and use this as your guide.

BELOW — By using a dial caliper, the height of the bosses can be checked, both before and after cutting them with the spot facer. The cut boss should measure out to exactly .55-inch high.

ABOVE — The stock Ford 351 rocker assembly is on the left. Note fulcrum stand. Beefier Manley set-up is on the right without adjuster.

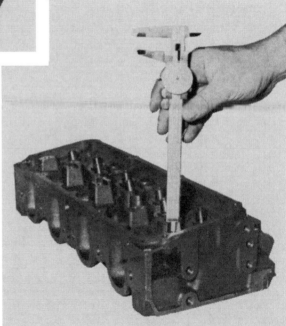

ABOVE — The spot facer used to cut down the bosses is available on a loan basis for $15. The pilot is 3/8-inch, and the same pilot hole is used to tap to 7/16-inch for the studs. BELOW — The stand (circle) is completely eliminated. Arrows show both an uncut and a faced boss. If tab remains after milling, then file off.

BELOW — This shot shows the stock setup on left and completed Manley assembly on the right. Note guide plate and how it is installed, and that the hardened tip of pushrod is up (arrow).

Text and photos by John Dianna ■ The stout 351 Cleveland engine is without a doubt one of the most popular in Ford's current engine line-up. Of course its being made available in nearly all of Ford's popular models is helping with its acceptance. As is the case with many of today's modern reciprocating engines equipped with hydraulic lifters, the 351 Cleveland has no provisions for adjusting valve lash. This of course is a problem if a guy desires to modify his engine and install a solid-lifter-type camshaft.

Designwise, the Cleveland head is excellent. The engineers responsible have incorporated rocker arm bosses that act not only as rocker arm supports but also as rocker arm guides. The bases of the rocker arm fulcrums are squared so that they mount directly into machined recesses at the tops of the bosses. Suprisingly, as simple as the design is, it's just as easy to modify the heads so that the rockers are adjustable. Basically what's required is to machine away the rails, drill and tap the shortened bosses and install a Manley MD 154 K rocker arm kit. Other pieces needed are a set of screw-in studs (MD 103), guide plates (MD 156) and pushrods (CM 752).

The kit is made up of 16 rocker arms, 16 fulcrums (rocker arm balls) and 16 self-locking nuts. To install the screw-in studs, a spot-facer tool (VST 1860) is available from Manley on a rental basis, with the deposit money ($15) refundable on the return of the tool. Other tools that are necessary to complete the job are an electric drill, a ⅜-inch drill bit and a 7/16-inch tap. To really do the job properly, the bosses should be drilled, using a drill press so that the angle of all the studs is maintained. For those of you on a budget, the installation can be completed with the simplest of tools (see accompanying photos).

The first step is to drill the existing 5/16-inch holes with a ⅜-inch drill bit. For a depth figure, measure the stock 5/16-inch holes (for example, our heads were 1.265 inches deep) and drill the ⅜-inch holes to that depth. This way you are sure that the spot-facer pilot doesn't bottom out and that you remove the required amount of material off the tops of the bosses. It's no big problem if you happen to drill too deep and break into the water passage, as the new screw-in studs coated with LocTite will seal off any seepage. Using the spot facer and an electric drill, reduce the bosses in height to a total figure of .550-inch (measured from an adjacent head bolt flange to the top of the boss). The stock heights will be in the neighborhood of .965-inch, which means about .415-inch of boss material must be removed. The reason for the removal of this material is the fact that you will be installing studs with an integral jam nut, plus a guide plate; and the studs need to be lowered so that they don't hit the rocker covers, the rockers don't bottom-out on the stud and the proper rocker arm geometry is maintained.

The next step is to tap the ⅜-inch holes to accept the screw-in studs, and at the time of the stud installation, also install Manley pushrod guide plates to accept the ⅜-inch diameter pushrods. The pushrod guide plates are needed because the rocker arms are no longer guided by the fulcrums. The stock pushrod holes machined in the heads are larger than the pushrods, so they too offer no rocker arm guidance. No additional modifications to the existing holes in the heads are necessary, as they are large enough to accept the bigger pushrods; however, it wouldn't hurt to double-check this clearance before firing the engine. The ⅜-inch Manley pushrods have long hardened ends that are designed to be used with the guide plates, so when the pushrods are installed, be sure to install the long tips so that they ride in the guide plates.

The installation should take about 40 minutes to complete, depending on the time you take checking each step. It's really an easy modification; and if any of you would like the advantage of increased rpm with a solid-lifter camshaft, don't overlook the fact that solid lifters require adjusting. Hank Manley didn't. ■ ■

Only one of the Ford 351-cubic-inch V8 engines has a real future. It is the 351-C, and the "C" stands for Cleveland, which is where that engine is made. The other 351 is the 351-W, and "W" denotes that it is an engine built in the Windsor, Ontario, plant. The 351-W was a stopgap measure for Ford. They had no small-block engine with mid-300-cubic-inch displacement; but General Motors, Chrysler and American Motors did, and this was quite obviously costing Ford a few customers. So for 1969, Ford released an expanded version of the 289-302 series V8 with 351 cubic inches. By the 1970 model year, the addition to their Cleveland Engine Plant No. 2 was completed, and the new design 351 was ready for production. But it took the combined supply of both Cleveland and Windsor plants to keep up with the anticipated demands for this size engine. This is why there is a mixture of 351-W and -C engines in the Ford line. In 1971, the Windsor engine will be used only in the big Fords, and then only in two-barrel carburetor form. While the Cleveland engine is inherently better in design and potential than the Windsor pattern, it is released for production with a good many compromises. The stock hydraulic cam has a .430-inch intake lift and .450-inch exhaust lift. Intake valve opening duration is 268°, exhaust is 280° and overlap is a scant 37°. The canted valve arrangement is a good idea, but for reasons of production and ease of assembly, a cylindrical fulcrum is used to hold the individual,

PUT-ONS for FORD of CLEVELAND

The "good" Ford 351 engine is going into its second year. Its birthday present is a few muscle parts

Text and photos by Steve Kelly

1) Here is special top plate made to accept Autolite In-Line (1 11/16-inch throttle bores) on single-carb intake with plenum chamber. 2) John Brown makes change to test engine's carburetion. 3) Offenhauser Power-Port intake with a pair of 710 cfm Holleys. Tubes leading into float bowls are connected to alcohol reservoir. Setup is used to richen mixture from dyno control room and see quickly whether or not mix is right. This manifold doesn't like low engine speeds. 4) Pair of Autolite In-Line carbs on special intake (2¼-inch throttle bores) really put out the power on ninth test. Ak felt a 50-percent reduction in stack height would be even better. 5) The 351-C received another set of Autolite In-Line carbs, and these were run without benefit of velocity stacks; didn't fare too badly.

16

stamped-steel rockers in place. The cylindrical fulcrum allows rocker arm movement, and the square boss on the bottom side of this fulcrum fits into the machined slot on the pedestal, which is part of the head casting. The square boss prevents rocker arm twisting or movement. No studs are used to mount the rockers to the head. A cap screw is all that's needed, since the pedestal height is enough to ensure good rocker arm attachment strength.

The Cleveland rocker arm design is truly a good one for production engines, but it hampers installation of a mechanical cam. Adjustable pushrods will not work well because, with a high-lift cam, the hex on the rod will strike the inside tip of the rocker. The adjustable rods could be turned upside down, and will work that way, but this means removing the intake manifold to adjust valve lash. Another

alternative is to use special studs (which were made up for dyno tests we'll discuss farther on) and make special pushrod guide plates. This is expensive. To use Boss 302 studs, guide plates and rocker fulcrums, the entire pedestal area would have to be machined from the Cleveland heads. Due to the canted angle of the valves, which dictates canting the pedestals, this also would be a costly and time-consuming operation. Adjustable rocker arms would be a natural substitution, but none are presently made. However, several equipment makers are going to introduce these as soon as they can complete design and tooling work. Unless you want to invest a lot of money in a Cleveland head right now, stick with the hydraulic cam until new rocker arms are on the market.

Autolite and the Ford Special Vehicles men worked over the 351 Cleveland quite extensively this summer to develop a few low-cost and effective muscle parts. The bulk of the testing was accomplished by Ak Miller at the Autolite Dyno Facility in Long Beach. Ak started out with an engine which had been run in for a six-hour break-in and check operation, and found that the out-of-the-crate engine performed about as he had expected: weak. It carries an in-the-car rating of 300 horsepower at 5400 rpm, and torque rating of 380 lbs.-ft. at 3400 rpm. This is the 4V engine, and compression is rated 11.0:1. It pulled to a maximum of 288 horsepower at 5200 rpm, with torque of 338 lbs.-ft. at 3400 rpm. Engine speed couldn't be increased safely past 5500 rpm, because valve bounce occurred at 5600 rpm.

In step two, Ak substituted a Holley 780 cfm (3310 model) carb for the stock Autolite 4300 4V, which is rated at 600 cfm. In order to use the 780 Holley, manifold inlets had to be milled out to allow the larger throttle plates to clear the manifold openings. Peak torque with this test was 351 lbs.-ft. at 3400 rpm, and horsepower was bumped to 297 at 5200 rpm. This step resulted in a very marginal increase for the effort and expense, but a larger carburetor is mandatory if other horsepower improvements are to be made. Just before bolting the 780 Holley in place, Ak compared the Autolite carburetor with a Holley 600 cfm model, and the Autolite 4300 was able to let the engine obtain about four more horses than the Holley. The air-valve operation on the Autolite allowed a smoother transition through the initial stages of secondary operation, while the 600 cfm secondary plates wanted to flutter a great deal at this point. At one point, the secondary plates started to flutter so badly the dyno looked like a paint shaker.

The third dyno test involved a change to the camshaft only. A semi-high-performance hydraulic cam, a prototype from Ford, with .500-inch lift and 290° intake duration and 300° exhaust opening duration, was used here. The 780 Holley remained in place, and everything else was stock. Torque jumped to a peak 354 lbs.-ft. at 3400 rpm, yet was the same right up to 5000. Horsepower peaked at 5800 rpm, and the reading was 340. Engine speed was still smooth at 5800 rpm. The engineering number is 47964 on this universal use (street and/or strip) shaft, yet no parts numbers have been assigned. In other words, it can't be ordered until someone at Ford decides this is the right way to go.

The fourth test was to determine if a larger carb could be justified with this cam. The result was that it couldn't. A Holley 850 double-pumper with mechanical secondaries was positioned atop the cast iron intake, and torque reading dropped a very slight amount to 3600-3800 rpm, yet was the same as in the previous test at 354 lbs.-ft. Horsepower increased to 347 at 5800 rpm, but the larger carburetor narrowed the torque band, in spite of its being responsible for a few more horses. Torque declined rapidly on each side of the peak point in relation to the 780 Holley test. Incidentally, an aluminum intake manifold for the 351-C will soon be available from Ford, if it isn't already. It has the same general configuration as the cast iron unit, but throttle-bore openings are larger to accommodate bigger carbs.

For the fifth test, another hydraulic cam profile was tried. It has the same .500-inch lift as the first, but shorter duration (about 10°) on both intake and exhaust. It showed a peak horsepower figure of 333 at 5800 rpm, but torque moved to 361 lbs.-ft. at 3800. The torque band with this cam is extremely wide, being strong from 3000 to 4400 rpm. In a sense, it follows production cams with its wide torque range, and this one probably has more promise for release as a muscle part than the other hydraulic stick.

The sixth test utilized a mechanical cam. This is where special studs (7/16-diameter bottom threads, 5/16-inch top) were used. Overall profile of this solid-lifter cam is similar to the first hydraulic cam tested, with duration over 300°, and with .520-inch lift. It carries street operating capabilities by having fairly tolerable idle speeds around 800-1000 rpm. Valve springs were taken from 429 C-J assembly, they being 10-15 lbs. more at the seat pressure than stock 351-C springs. Ninety pounds spring pressure at the seat is stock specs for both intake and exhaust. This cam showed a very wide torque band, running smoothly from 3000 to 4400 rpm, and peak torque was 366 lbs.-ft. at 3800 rpm. Horsepower topped at 366 at 6200 rpm, and horsepower fell off quickly at 6400 rpm. Valve toss entered at 6800 rpm.

The seventh run included switching to the 850 cfm Holley again, and placing a two-inch riser plate between it and the manifold. This hurt low-speed horsepower, as well as mid-range, and though power is equal at the top end, this test proved a deficiency in design. The riser plate used was an open one, which integrates all four runners directly below the carburetor. If you're going to use a riser plate, get one with individual openings for each carburetor bore.

The eighth test involved a switch to an open-plenum, dual four-barrel aluminum manifold and a pair of Holley 710 cfm carbs. This manifold is not for release. It is only a prototype. Low-speed operation proved out very poor, and the engine didn't start to work until 5000 rpm. It was all through at 6600 rpm, which is also the point of most horse-power: 398. Peak torque was achieved at 5000 rpm: 346 lbs.-ft. This was the only good torque reading along the engine speed pattern, and torque was diminished to a very weak point by the time horsepower was rising. Valve toss was evident just past 6600 rpm, and Ak feels that valve springs with 30 to 40 pounds more pressure would've helped considerably.

The ninth test was the best. A pair of 2¼-inch throttle-bore Autolite In-Lines were attached to the engine by way of a specially fabricated intake manifold. Seven-and-a-half-inch-tall velocity stacks were slipped over the inlets, though Ak advises that stacks half that height should be used for better torque and sustained horsepower. Anyway, the torque peaked out at 4800 rpm, and the corrected reading was 376 lbs.-ft. It pulled evenly all the way up to its peak point, and horsepower was identical to the dual-four setup (398 at 6600 rpm). But the difference was low-speed idling, and the dual Autolite system would properly idle at 600 rpm. Low-speed operation was very good and termed fantastic by Ak in comparison to the dual-four inlet.

Ollie Morris visited Ak for a few days at the dyno, bringing along the latest Offenhauser Power Port manifold for a few trials on the 351. Matched pairs of Holley 600, 710 and 780 cfm-rated carbs were tried on the tall-runner aluminum intake, with the 710s proving best on the 351 with mechanical cam. The best horsepower reading was 358 at 6200 rpm, and torque reached a maximum of 364 lbs.-ft. at 4800 rpm. It carries its torque climb very well, and the high-torque band is very wide. Power is observed as low as 3400 rpm, but this induction method is almost devoid of idling possibilities. Top end power doesn't diminish rapidly. This method of carburetion qualifies well for drag racing.

The front cover on a 351-C is like that of the small-block Chevy, only the "C" cover is a flat plate. Dowels on top line it up, and it lips under and into the oil pan. This means cam changes can be a nuisance, and unlike the Chevy cover, the Ford cover won't bend. After you've struggled and fought to get the cover off once, file the pan lip edges a small amount before replacing it. Then it'll go on — and come off — easier, and all you have to remember is to be generous with the gasket sealant around the pan/cover contact.

The stock distributor is a single-point unit with vacuum advance features. It is good for no more than 5500 rpm before point bounce sends the spark in too many directions. A dual-plate unit with mechanical advance action and 28-ounce springs are needed; and this is exactly what Autolite has proposed, packaged, but so far not released. The dual-point plate simply slips in, and cost of the total kit is somewhere around $10. The kit has been ready for a number of months now, but powers within Autolite have cast the thing into a state of limbo. Guess the fact that it would sell doesn't mean very much.

The bottom end of the 351 Cleveland 4-bbl motor is not in need of help, but for those who would like to increase main bearing strength, aftermarket bearing suppliers such as TRW, Federal-Mogul and Clevite do have heavy-duty main bearings. Rod journal bearings are fine for all but the most severe uses.

A Holley 780 cfm-carbed 351 Cleveland, on an enlarged-opening intake, with either of the two hydraulic cams, is good for high-13-second quarter-mile e.t.s in a Mustang. This is with a 3.50 gear and stock exhausts. The cams (one or possibly both) will be part of a new muscle parts book supplement out soon, and there'll even be a new low-cost Autolite carburetor with flow capability of 780 cfm. You know from the tests how exotic you can get on a 351-C, and also how simple it is to start it churning out horsepower. It doesn't take much. ■■

Interior look at Offenhauser Power-Port intake. Notches in center dividers are for throttle plate clearance. Later tests showed removing dividers didn't change output at all.

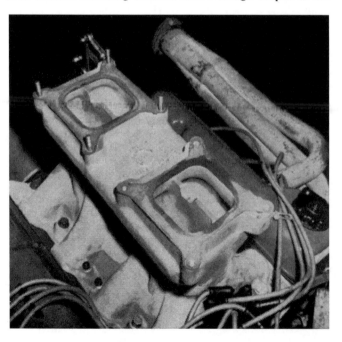

Making the 351 BOSS

The current state of the art for Pinto Pro motors

by Steve Collison

The demand for high-performance talent at Ford these days is exceeded only by that for aerospace workers on the West Coast. In other words, business is slow.

In spite of total factory withdrawal from all facets of motorsports, there still are those daring young men who continue to run their Fords. And as far as drag racing is concerned, that tenacity has dammed the mainstream of things—particularly the three-year domination of Pro Stock by Chrysler and Chevrolet. But since the outset of the '73 season, Fords have placed at more major NHRA meets than all other brands combined. Spearheading this now completely independent effort are Don Nicholson, Ken Dondero, Gapp & Roush, Glidden & Allen and, most recently, Don Grotheer.

Perhaps most instrumental in the research and development of the Boss 351 for drag racing are ex-Ford engineers Wayne Gapp and Jack Roush. When race budgets were cut back and then dropped altogether, factory performance people like Gapp and Roush retired to modest buildings on the outskirts of Detroit to devote their time and effort toward the preservation of the Boss 351 for Pro Stock.

Of course, when you work for an auto maker in engine development and manufacturing, certain information and parts connections are readily available. Wayne and Jack were careful not to burn any bridges and escaped to the suburbs with the last of many good pieces that were originally designed specifically for their application. And now that Ford's Off Highway Only parts program also has folded, neat things like aluminum water pumps, stiffer oil pump springs and trick lightweight valves are next to impossible to come by.

Whereas the Chrysler Pro Stock contingent relies almost exclusively on factory-developed parts, the Ford camp was split into what some called the "California combination" and the "factory way." Nicholson was responsible for achieving his performance levels through heavy usage of the California aftermarket industry, while Gapp & Roush trusted factory components and information. Now that their source has been all but exhausted, the Midwest Ford Pro Stock racers are "looking to the West" for help. This means that more consistent parts are being used throughout everyone's motors. And, because Gapp & Roush build 80% of the Pro Stock Pinto engines and a fair share of Modified renditions, what could be more representative of the current state of the art than to take a tour through one of their 152 mph Boss 351's? Remember that the following information applies to Modified Production and those classes accepting unlimited internal alterations in AHRA and IHRA.

(Please forgive the following continued comparisons between Ford's 351 Cleveland engine and Chevrolet's Mark IV series of big-blocks, but many feel the Ford to be a scaled-down version of the 427 Chevy, a fact never officially repudiated by those in the know at Dearborn.)

Generally, the Boss 351 has its good and bad points. The cylinder head is as efficient as any unwelded rat motor unit but weighs a hefty 52 pounds. In fact, an entire 351C motor is within 20 pounds of an aluminum-headed big-block Chevy. Another detriment for racing is the block itself. While the thin wall casting process benefits cooling, those same thin walls present a problem when core shifts further reduce their thickness. Cracked cylinder walls are common when the block is opened up .020 inches for Pro Stock application. But a good mark is logged for Ford's penchant for sealing, as the Cleveland engines are virtually airtight.

To begin with, Gapp & Roush suggest you forget anything you may have heard about the Boss 351 and its dependability. They have an engine at the shop that hasn't missed a beat in over 100 sprints down the quarter mile, so one might say they've found the secret to longevity.

CYLINDER BLOCK and OILING

While Gapp & Roush use the standard 4-inch bore, 4-bolt main 351C block, they have successfully run the 2-bolt version without difficulty. The main caps for both blocks are identical, save for the number of bolts and their placement. We mention this because the 2-bolt main block is cheaper and easier to find.

After selecting whichever casting suits you, G & R recommend the usual deburring and a radius around the main journal area at the bottom of each cylinder. They then "Siamese" the two oil return holes nearest the rear of the block in the valley area to promote runoff and "scallop" the intake and exhaust sections at the tops of the cylinders, using a head gasket as a template (see photos).

You may recall the bearing problems encountered by Nicholson when he first began running the 351. After umpteen spun bearings and burnt cranks it was discovered that his aftermarket oil pump was to blame. Gapp & Roush have always used the stock Boss pump but in conjunction with certain modifications to the block's oiling system.

On an engine spinning at over 9000 rpm, maintaining sufficient lubrication to the crankshaft and main bearings is most critical. To promote more efficient oiling to these areas in the 351 Cleveland, the oil galley running from the rear main to the left hand lifter galley is restricted with a ⅜-inch section of coarse threaded rod that is slotted at one end for installation (like a metering jet) and drilled with a .080-inch orifice to cut down on excessive valve train lubrication. Each of the cam bearings gets a similar plug made from 5/16-inch coarse rod and a .060-inch hole. There is

no need to drill and tap the front cam bearing, as it is fed from another source and is OK as is. The stock Boss 351 oil pump is then fitted with a heavy-duty spring (P/N D2ZX6670AA) to boost line pressure. G & R claim 125 psi with a cold engine and approximately 60-70 psi at 8000 rpm once she's warm. Oil pan capacity is 9 quarts.

Depending on the size of the engine they are building, Jack will bore the block .020 inches for a total of 354 cubic inches or leave it standard for use with stock pistons. In either case, G & R use a torque plate and head gasket firmly attached to the block to prevent cylinder flex during the honing process. The last .005 inch is removed with a #820 Sunnen stone to assure concentricity.

CRANKSHAFT ASSEMBLY

The stock Boss unit receives only limited attention. Assuming it's straight, the crank is chucked up in a lathe and widened at the rod journals to accept 327-350 Chevy 2.1-inch bearings (TRW P/N CB826P). Aside from tuftriding, the only remaining operation is enlarging the oil holes to a quarter-inch.

Gapp & Roush credit the aluminum rod as the single most important piece in their motors. Jack states that steel rods have a tendency to "bite" the crank and spin bearings at low oil temperatures. The aluminum version is best for cold engines, negating warmup time and allowing the motor to be "blipped"

as soon as oil pressure has built up. The rod employed is a Brooks Racing Component measuring 6.070 inches versus the 5.875-inch standard length. G & R purchase the rods in unfinished form so they can juggle bore-to-stroke combinations by finish-machining the small end themselves.

Piston choice is a 13.0:1 BRC aluminum item weighing 595 grams with a full floating Teflon-buttoned wrist pin. Each piston is fitted with .062-inch compression rings—a moly top and ductile iron second—and a ⅛-inch oiler, all from Sealed Power.

Contrary to normal procedure, the Gapp & Roush Boss 351 is internally balanced within the block, rather than on the outside via the flywheel and harmonic balancer (ala

Most Pinto Pro motors today look just like this one, a "Boss 354" built by Gapp & Roush.

Edelbrock/Holley 4500 induction combo requires manifold be trimmed .4 inch for hood clearance.

Much of engine's horsepower is derived from high-port exhaust and aluminum spacer plate, used to clean up valve angle.

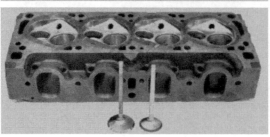

Intake side of head is tunnel-ported and fitted with hard-to-come-by, lightweight Ford valves. Polished combustion chambers hold 59 cc's each.

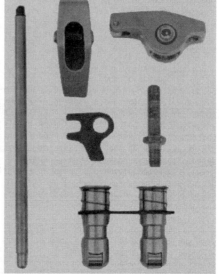

Valvetrain is made up of Smith Bros. pushrods, G-K cam and rockers, Manley guide plates cut in half, stock studs and Crane lifters.

Long 6.070-inch Brooks rod and Teflon-buttoned pin swing either TRW or BRC 13:1 pistons.

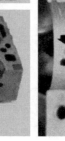

Galley feeding cam bearings is restricted with plugs made from threaded rod for better oiling to main bearings.

454 Chevy). It's not a difficult operation, especially after the crank journals have been widened and the aluminum rods added. The crank counterweights are drilled and filled with mallory, a very dense and expensive alloy, to offset the piston/rod mass. Switching to an aftermarket flywheel and machining the stock balancer to bring it back to a non-counterweighted condition complete the process. This is not recommended for street applications using steel rods and stock crankshafts, because the normal car owner would go broke buying enough mallory to compensate for those stock pieces. It is, however, a necessary function for Pro Stock and serious Modified competitors.

CYLINDER HEADS

As mentioned earlier, the stock Boss casting is very effective, due largely to its canted valve design and shallow combustion chambers. But, by the time you add multiple carburetion and a high-lift Pro Stock camshaft, the head's breathing capabilities are sorely taxed. The logical step is to contour both the intake and exhaust ports to "set up" an increase in air flow.

When Jack does a set of customer's heads, he specifies the use of brand-new castings to insure fresh valve guides. He then adds 11/32-inch Chevy valve seals to the intakes only, having noted zero oiling and guide wear on the exhausts after 75 runs.

Next in line are the ports themselves. The intake side is tunnel-ported and polished—nothing really trick. But the exhausts are a bit different since the original passage was a compromise for use with cast iron exhaust manifolds in assorted body styles. The scavenging side of the head is ported, polished and re-contoured (a fancy term for cutting open and welding closed a runner) to properly align the newly raised port with the custom-made aluminum exhaust plate (see "Cut and Paste Ports," February '73 CC). The raised exhaust really cleans up the valve angle, but may present a problem in some cars where the spacer comes close to or actually hits the shock towers. Headers for those applications are a tad trick.

Extensive work in the combustion chamber area is precluded by polishing and milling .010 inch off the intake side for manifold fit once the entire head has been surfaced. Valve work consists of seat widths of .060 inch on the intake, .070 on the exhaust; while approach, seat and valve angles are 20, 44 and 75 degrees, respectively, for both sides.

The valves used are the factory race items nobody has. The intakes (DOZX6507A) are hollow stem/stainless steel with 11/32-inch stems and 2.19-inch head diameters. The sodium-filled exhausts measure 1.71 inch and can be found under DOZX6505A (maybe). Gapp & Roush suggest you try Ford 427 medium riser valves if the Pro Stock pieces can't be located. They have ⅜-inch stems and must be shortened about .100 inch to fit the Boss heads, so they will work in a pinch.

The five-fold head gasket is yet another special Ford item (D3ZX6051AA), consisting of one sheet asbestos, two each of composition and a like amount of steel layers, all sandwiched for a compressed thickness of .038 inch.

VALVE TRAIN

The heart of Gapp & Roush's valve train beats with a General Kinetics roller cam containing 321 degrees duration and .721 inch lift on the intake, and 330 degrees and .700 inch of similar happenings on the exhaust. G-K also supplies the 1.65:1 roller rockers and dual valve springs that are installed at 180 psi closed and 525 psi open. Smith Brothers hardened tip pushrods ride on Manley guide plates that have been cut in half to align with the stock Boss studs. Crane roller lifters complete the valvetrain assembly.

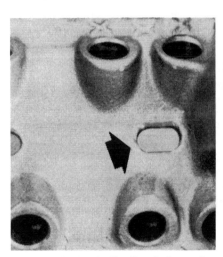

Also contributing to the Boss's longevity is additional oil to camshaft via merger of last two runoff holes in valley.

Stock Boss crank is widened at main bearing journals for use with small-block Chevy bearings, then tuftrided and balanced internally. Oil holes are enlarged to ¼-inch for efficient flow.

INDUCTION

Lighting the Boss 351's fire is Accel's new Breakerless Electronic Ignition kit (BEI) with a 5-degree curve, 10 degrees initial timing and a total of 40 degrees at 2000 rpm. Champion is the plug choice. Their BL-3, BL-60Y or BL-62Y units are employed, depending on weather conditions.

CLEARANCES

In the event you plan to tackle what we've laid out for you, Gapp & Roush recommend the following engine clearances: aluminum rod side clearance—.030 inch; main bearing—.004; rod bearing—.003; piston skirt-to-wall—(TRW) .005 and .010 inch (BRC); top and second ring end gaps—.015 and .012-inch, respectively.

Deck height with the aluminum rods is suggested at .025 inch down in the hole as measured on the flat portion of the piston dome. Even though they run the Lenco trans, piston-to-valve clearance is held to .100 on the intake and .140 on the exhaust.

There you have it. Everything you need to know in order to build your very own 650 hp Boss motor. The information can be applied to the 302 as well, so don't think you have to use the 351 exclusively. If you happen to be the lazy type, Gapp & Roush Performance will gladly supply a complete twin to their highly successful combination for a mere $5500. Buying the heads alone (about $800) and doing the work yourself will afford considerable monetary savings—and you can be assured the finished product will definitely fly. ⦿

If aluminum Boss 351 water pump is not available at your dealer, try ordering the early 289 hi-po model (C50Z8501A). Adapter at right is Gapp & Roush piece needed to mate pump to Boss block.

Surprisingly, the only modification made to original Boss pump is adding a high-pressure spring (D2ZX6670AA).

Ford's attention has shifted to the small-block and these new parts will help make the difference

BY STEVE COLLISON ■ For those of you who haven't heard, Ford is back in racing. At least in terms of over-the-counter replacement parts. While at their new-car preview this summer, Ford turned us on to an informative booklet available FREE from the Detroit facility. It's chock full of factory suggestions on chassis set-up, parts interchangeability for most of their engines, comprehensive assembly instructions and even "go fast" tips for 4 and 6-cylinder motors. To get your very own copy, write to: Off Highway Parts Book, Milwaukee Junction Station, P.O. Box 5386, Detroit, Mich. 48211.

The following is a brief glimpse and explanation of some of the better Boss 351 parts available from Ford, a few of which are not listed in the O.H.O. (Off Highway Only) book. They are presented here as harbingers of a rash of Boss parts to be featured on these pages in coming months.

The "Boss" family of small-block Fords is often compared to the Chevrolet 396-427-454 series because of their similar canted valve head configuration and scaled-down block castings. One improvement by Ford engineers in the Boss 351 cylinder head allows it to "breathe" more ef-

The Dearborn Shuffle

Stock external balance damper is at left with counterweight intact. Ford recommends machining for drag racing conversions.

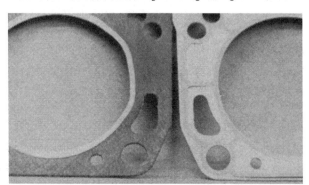

The old .046-inch head gasket on left has been redesigned for better sealing. Newer .036-inch compressed gasket is at right.

TRW replacement piston necessitates .030-inch overbore, needs fire-slot cut into dome. Super-duty stock rod and tapered pin are hot tip.

fectively at high rpm. The solution stemmed from an aluminum spacer that bolts to the exhaust side of the head to move the port higher to enhance air flow from the combustion chamber. It's similar to that used on Don Nicholson's Pinto but can be had only from Bud Moore, 400 N. Fairview, Spartanburg, S.C. 29302. The spacer and cylinder head *must* be purchased as an assembly because of the special machine work involved. A nice thing about the spacer is that stock headers will bolt right up. The accompanying photos show both side and cross-sectional views of the spacer which must be used with 1/2-inch-by-13 bolts of Grade 8 quality. A hardened washer under the bolt is another necessity to prevent damaging the aluminum spacer.

While on the subject of heads, another shortcoming noticed by Ford engineers was in the area of proper sealing. The old head gaskets had a compressed thickness of .046 inches and were prone to leakage. A new gasket, carrying part number D3ZZ6051-A, helps boost compression with a .036-inch thickness. Its matrix-type construction stems from an asbestos sandwich having a metal core. The replacement also resists aeration, due to different designing, around the cylinder and water passages. Torque recommendations for racing are 125 ft./lbs. HOT.

The next item is Ford's trick lightweight titanium intake valve for both the 302 and 351 Boss engines. Weighing just 85 grams, it has a hardened cap welded to the tip for increased durability, and a moly-coated stem ending in a swirl-polished head measuring 2.19 inches in diameter. Reported to be good for 9000 rpm in a 302, the titanium valve has a flat seat and must be used in heads having other than a radiused seat. Total valve length is 5.23 inches. Part number is DOZX6507-A.

Need more oil pressure in that race motor? A high-tension oil pump spring for the stock pump will boost the pressure up to 90 psi for added dependability. Just step up to the parts counter and ask for D2ZX6670-AA.

Since all Boss 351's are externally balanced through counterweighted dampers and flywheels, it is advisable to convert these items to the more efficient internal balance, especially for high-rpm applications. First, secure damper D1ZZ6316-B. Machine out the counterweighted section as pictured (any reputable machine shop can handle this operation). The remaining thorn in your side is the stock flywheel. Assuming the motor is going quick enough to facilitate the use of an aftermarket clutch assembly, pick up a non-stock, non-weighted flywheel as well.

Ford recommends a .030-inch overbore TRW replacement piston for the Boss 351, carrying TRW part number L2348 + .030. Rated at 12.5:1 compression, the piston needs to have a "fire slot" notched into the dome to improve flame propagation. It may also have to be flycut for proper piston-to-valve clearance when used with the higher lift camshafts. Deck heights should be run .010 inches below the block for optimum compression.

In conjunction with the TRW piston, the Ford Boss 351 connecting rod and stock pressed and tapered wrist pin are the ideal combination.

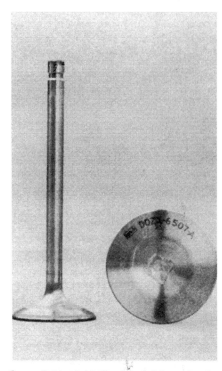

Super-lightweight titanium intake valve for Boss 302 and 351 is just 85 grams, is OK for 9000 rpm. Diameter is 2.19 inches.

The rod itself is really a sturdy piece, machined from SAE 1041 steel and then shotpeened and magnafluxed for durability. The strong 3/8-inch rod bolts can withstand pressures up to 180,000 psi and both are good for 7500 rpm in stock form. For drag racing, the rods should undergo polishing and another shotpeen (in that order) before their big ends are reconditioned to correct distortion and to increase bearing crush. The additional work is required to conform with an increase in torque specifications from 45-50 to 55 ft./lbs.

It's nice to have someone else doing all the flog work when it comes to sorting out which parts are best for a particular application. From the information we've received, Ford is making a concentrated effort to regain some of the lost limelight in the performance market. With parts like these, they'll be needing sunglasses in Dearborn. Remember, Dyno Don broke all of those engines for YOU! Ⓖ

Bud Moore aluminum spacer is truly a trick piece, adds as much as 25 hp to Boss 351 cylinder heads, accepts stock headers.

New oil pump spring ups pressure to 90 psi.

1

AK'S ATTACK

HOW THE WORLD'S OLDEST HOT RODDER BUILDS A 351 FORD TO PROVE WHO'S *BOSS* AT PIKE'S PEAK.

BY JAY STORER

It's not that Ak Miller is ready for the wheelchair or anything, he's only 51 years old, it's just that he's been a hot rodder, in every sense of the term, for longer than just about anybody. There may be others around who were racing before Ak did, but Ak is *still* building hot rods, racing cars, and driving like a hot rodder!

Ak's personal history in hot rodding is so long and colorful, we could easily devote a whole book to the subject. His first car, a '28 Chevy 4-cylinder roadster, was also his first hot rod, not unsurprisingly. He was 15 at the time. Shortly after the war, Ak really got into the competition scene, which at the time was dry lakes racing. And in the late '40's, he scored his first win in a competitive

2

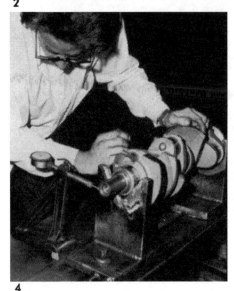

4

5

1. Ak Miller pushes the Chaffee College Mustang around corner on famous Pike's Peak, dirt-trackin' his way to a first in the production class in 1971 race.

2. First step in any engine build-up is a thorough cleaning of the block. Ak Miller washes the block with water and solvent to clean out any residue left from the machining operations at Reath Automotive, who surfaced the deck and honed the cylinders.

3. John Meyer, a machinist at the Ak Miller Garage, watches as the "old man" checks the cylinder taper with gauge.

4. Machinist at Reath Automotive is here checking Ak's iron crankshaft for straightness, measuring the runout at the nose and main bearing journals.

5. After determining that the crank was "in the ballpark," the oil holes were chamfered (arrows) and all the journals were "micropolished."

6

7

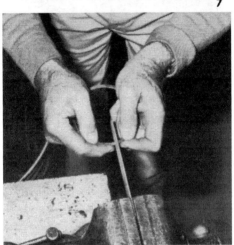

8

9

event with a highboy roadster. Through the years, Ak has raced sports cars, sprint cars, drag cars, road racers, and Bonneville cars, and he usually did an inordinate amount of winning, to boot.

Engines of just about every make have run in competition with the Ak Miller touch, but mostly Fords. So it seemed only natural when Ford got back into racing in 1962, that Ak was selected to be Ford Performance Advisor, a position he still holds today while still running his busy auto repair and tune-up shop (9225 Slauson Ave., Pico Rivera, Calif.).

Of all the kinds of racing he has been involved in, Ak's personal favorite is the annual Pike's Peak Hill Climb, which is the second oldest auto race still running. It's one of the most demanding races in the world, of the driver as well as the car. The 13-mile course up the mountain *begins* at an altitude of 9000 ft., and follows a twisty, 25-ft. wide dirt road up to the summit, some 14,110 ft. up! Some pretty thin air up there. The average engine is losing about 45% of its power by the time it gets to the top. Ak calls it "the great equalizer," because "there are 165 corners to make mistakes on." Since it's dirt racing, the tires are spinning madly all the time and drifting the corners. You lose 1/32-in. of your rear tire tread for every mile of the race! You run at high rpm's at all times and there's

6. Ak says the average guy can check his clearances with Plastigage, but since he has the tools, he prefers using micrometers. With the bearings in place and the caps torqued down, he measures the inside diameter. He then mikes the crank, and the difference is the clearance, .0025 to .0030-in. on mains, and rods.

7. Desired crankshaft end-play, which is measured by prying on crank while a dial indicator is attached at the flywheel face, is .004-.010-in.

8. Squaring a ring in the cylinder, Ak checks the ring end-gap with a feeler gauge. Rings are chromed items made by Perfect Circle.

9. If gap isn't the desired .015-in. the rings have to be filed. They have to be filed squarely, so Ak puts the file in a vise and runs ring back and forth in a straight line.

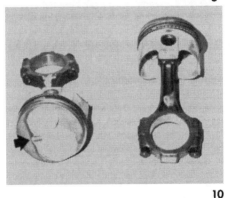

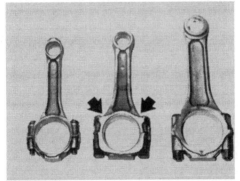

10

11

10. The Boss 051 rods have plenty of beef for competition. Pistons used are also stock Boss items (made for Ford by TRW), but Ak has cut .060-in. valve reliefs because of high-lift cam used. The fireslot (arrow) has also been deepened.

11. At left is a stock 302 rod, while in the center is a Boss 351 with stronger rod bolt area (where most rod failures occur). Just for comparison, rod at right is a big-block Chevy.

12

12. The area around the bolt head is the most important part of a rod. At left is a stock 302 rod, which has a straight broach cut, while the Boss 302 (center) has a radiused cut, as well as ⅜-in. bolts. The Boss 351 rod at right is identical, except for a longer stroke and larger bolts.

1

2

3

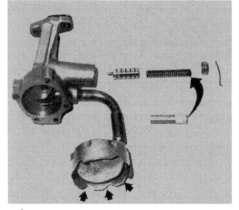

4

5

1. Ak oils rings thoroughly, puts a compressor on the piston and rings, and taps it into the cylinder with the aid of a rod bolt guide. You can also use rubber hoses for guides, to keep from nicking the crank journal.

2. Although Ak had checked his rod bearing clearances with a mike, it never hurts to doublecheck. If you can tap the rod and move it slightly side to side, clearance is ok.

3. With two rods installed on their journal, they can be pried to one side and the side clearance can be checked. On the Boss 351 it's .018-.022-in.

4. Ak makes three modifications to the Boss 351 oil pump (DOAZ6600B). The pickup tube is extended so the pickup will almost sit on the floor of the oil pan, and thus the pickup has cuts around it for oil entry. Since Ak uses an external oil system bypass, the pump's bypass spring is replaced with machined bolt or plug.

5. Be sure the little clip on the oil pump shaft is towards the block when you install it. It keeps the shaft from coming out of the oil pump when you pull the distributor.

6. The latest racing cam from Ford is this thumper, D1ZX-6250-FA; it comes with lifters. These lifters are radiused for use with this cam, and this .600-in. lift, 320° duration cam should not be used without them.

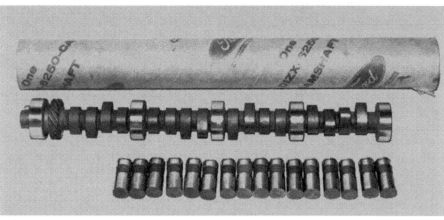

6

AK'S ATTACK

no such thing as too much horsepower. Speeds vary from as slow as 10 mph in tight places to 100 mph on stretches. In some places, it's like running on ice.

Ak got into racing at the Peak in 1958. He had just finished building a sports car which he was especially proud of. It was a Devin fiberglass body on a tube chassis he built himself out of seamless oilfield tubing; he ran a 340-in. Chevy with six 2-bbl. carburetors, and he had adapted a Chevy independent front end. Jerry Unser, father of Al and Bobby, was a friend of Ak's at the time, and after seeing the car, Jerry told Ak he was "chicken" if he didn't race at Pike's

Peak. So Ak trucked his car on up there and proceeded to win the unlimited sports car category in his first time on the hill. He's been hooked on it ever since, and in the past 14 years he's won eight times, and never finished further back than 6th in his class!

The subject engine of this article, a Boss 351 Ford, is to be installed in the 1970 Mustang owned by Chaffee College, Cerritos, Calif. The school uses the car as a rolling test lab for their students in the Race Car Technology course. They've been plagued with mechanical breakage, but otherwise have made a creditable showing in several Trans-Am races. Last year Ak borrowed the Mustang, swapped in his 351 and took it to Pike's Peak. His first time in the stock

car class and he did it to the troops with a winning 14 mins., 21 secs.

Ak will be running the car again this year for his 14th entry in the 4th of July racing classic. We were priviledged to follow, camera and notebook in hand, as Ak went through the engine in preparation for the Peak. Along the way we learned some things (you can't be around Ak Miller for more than 5 mins. without learning something) about engine design, chemistry, airflow characteristics and metallurgy, all subjects with which Ak is thoroughly experienced. Remember, through his long association with the engineers at Ford, Ak has had the advantages of being able to see theories tried out, tests performed, and myths exploded. For almost every area

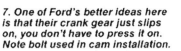

7. One of Ford's better ideas here is that their crank gear just slips on, you don't have to press it on. Note bolt used in cam installation.

8. The cam thrust plate can be installed two ways, either way is o.k.

9. Install the cam gear, eccentric and bolt without a chain so the end-play can be checked. Pull the cam back and forth to see if you have .001-.006-in. end-play (thrust).

10. Although Ak uses electric fuel pumps in his race car (the stock fuel pump mount on the engine is blocked off), the eccentric must still be used. The tab on the eccentric has to fit into the hole in the cam gear.

11. Since this engine is for racing only, future teardowns for cam changes are expected, so Ak uses 3M adhesive on the inside of the front cover's gasket, and wheel bearing grease on the cover side. This way the gasket will stay in one place and in one piece through several cam changes.

12. A windage tray is incorporated in the stock Boss oil pan and no other tray is needed. Ak deepened his from the stock 6 qts. to 8 qts.

13. Since no sealer is used on the pan gaskets, proper tightening is a must. But what this means is to avoid overtightening, which warps the pan.

14. Instead of stock head bolts, Ak had a set of studs made. The threads are rolled, and the studs are made of supertough metal so they can stand torquing, racing, and retorquing without stretch or fatigue.

of engine or chassis design under discussion, he can back up his statements with the results of tests conducted at one time or another by the engineering labs back in Dearborn. He's the kind of guy you can't win an argument with!

THE CAST IRON CRANK

Being somewhat renowned as a myth-exploder, Ak got us off to the right start on this engine story, exploding a few myths about crankshaft design. We were somewhat taken aback to find that this engine, built by a pro and destined for heavy abuse, was to use a *cast iron* crank! Most hot rodders make a big noise about steel cranks being a *must*, but Ak explained. "The average guy tends to believe everything he reads and hears from his buddies, and to a certain extent guys will construct a car or engine under the monkey-see-monkey-do method. If so-and-so uses a steel crank, well then it must be the answer. However, many of these same people lack a basic understanding of metallurgy. They don't know the basic differences between steel and cast iron."

We haven't got space enough for the technical detail that Ak goes into when he's wound up, but he did straighten us out on the properties of iron and steel. Steel may be stronger in many situations, but in the role of a crank there are many other considerations besides tensile strength. Modern casting technology produces strong iron parts, and the advantages of better oil retention, longwearing-surfaces, lower cost, and easier manufacturing and machining

9

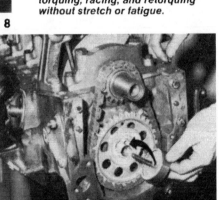

10

11

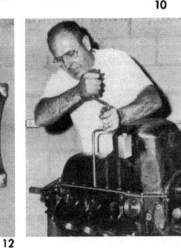

12

13

STUD WITH NUT AND WASHER

STOCK BOLT

14

1

2

make the cast iron crank a good idea. The iron in the Boss 351 crank is known as "select" cast iron, meaning that it has been especially selected for hardness and has a good 90% nodularity. It may surprise you to learn that Dyno Don Nicholson is using this same iron crank in his 351 Pinto Prostocker.

To return to the engine at hand, very little special preparation of the crank was required. Reath Automotive, Long Beach, Calif. checked it for straightness in a set of V-blocks. Then the oil holes in the journals were chamfered, and finally the journals were micro-polished, a procedure which removes less than .0005-in. and leaves a finish like chrome. At the same time, the block was precision-honed on a Sunnen Cylinder

1. There are tools made for putting studs in. But in this case Ak uses the tried-and-true double-nut method. The studs must be oiled first.

2. The strengths and weaknesses of the Boss heads were probed on a flow bench for concrete results. Here Ak looks on as Jerry Branch, of Branch Flowmetrics, Long Beach, Calif. checks out a Modello-ported head.

3. You can tell a lot about the air pumping characteristics of an engine with a flow bench. Here's the stock head compared to the ported one. Note how the stock intake port and valve level off in airflow at .650-in. lift while the ported head keeps going. See also how much more the porting helped the intake than the exhaust, which is the weak side of the Boss heads.

4. In airflow, it's not the size of the hole that counts, but the shape. The canted-valve design of Cleveland heads make for good intake angle, but the exhaust (below) has a bad hump to travel over, even though the port is bigger than on some engines.

5. Combustion chambers in the 302 heads were polished and cc'd. The 302 heads were used because they have a smaller combustion chamber volume than the 351 heads so it's easier to get high compression with them.

6. At left is the "trick" titanium intake valve (#DOZX-6507-A), center is a hollow 427-type, and at right is a stock Boss valve. Non-Boss valves have three keeper grooves for valve rotation. The titanium valve is the best for a competition engine.

7. The titanium valve is super-light, of course, but it also has a hardened steel tip and the stem is coated with molybdenum to reduce wear.

8. Special flat washers must be used under the nuts for the head studs. The valve springs, retainers and spring stands are all Ford competition parts. The "triple-spring" is actually two springs with a dampener.

9. The Ford competition rocker arm assembly is stronger, but slightly heavier than the aluminum aftermarket types. Note the varying kinds of stand used with the different rockers.

3

Flow chart:
- Y-axis: FLOW IN CUBIC FEET OF AIR (CFM), from 25 to 250
- X-axis: VALVE LIFT IN THOUSANDTHS, from 50 to 700
- Curves labeled: MODIFIED INTAKE, STOCK INTAKE PORT, MODIFIED EXHAUST, STOCK EXHAUST PORT

King, and again practically no metal was removed in the wall-finishing process.

SHORT-BLOCK TRICKS

As with any professionally-built engine, the preparation and assembly of the short block was an exercise in painstaking care. Ak is of the school that knows "cleanliness is next to Godliness" when it comes to assembling an engine. He also stressed at every step of the procedure the importance of proper lubrication during assembly. Everything that wasn't coated with Lubriplate was coated with either Isky Cam Lube or regular engine oil. Bearings recieved the Lubriplate treatment, the lifters and cam got the cam lube, and the rings, valve train and many other components were oiled. The break-in period is particularly important. If the engine hasn't been lubricated and assembled properly, it won't last very long when you first fire it up and run high rpm's on the dyno or in the car.

While we are on the subject of the short-block components, let's talk about another myth that the old master exploded for us. He had told us from the beginning that this engine would be built to obtain more than 500 hp with a single 4-bbl. and stock displacement, and all this with factory parts! We had been watching him all the way through the engine buildup, looking for him to slip some "trick" aftermarket part in while we weren't looking! It wasn't until the last bolt had been tightened on the completed engine that we realized Ak really *had* done the whole job with stock Ford parts. It's a testimony to the Ford engineers for staying on top of the racing scene through Ak and others who race Ford products.

MAKING HORSEPOWER

The point was really driven home to us

4

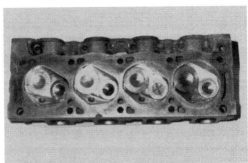

5

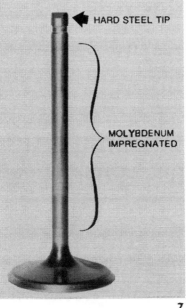

HARD STEEL TIP

MOLYBDENUM IMPREGNATED

7

8

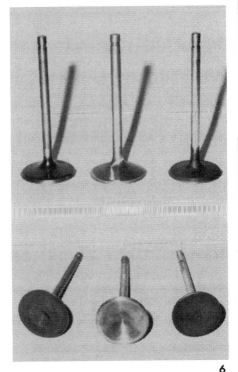

6

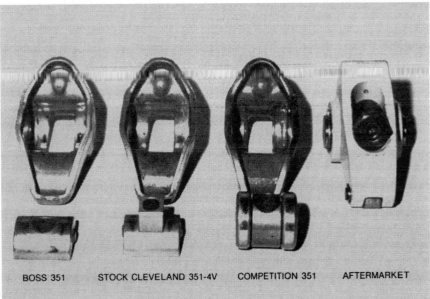

BOSS 351   STOCK CLEVELAND 351-4V   COMPETITION 351   AFTERMARKET

9

29

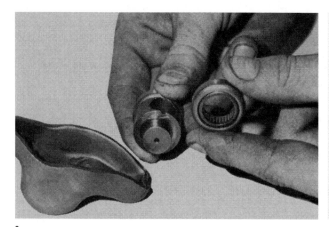
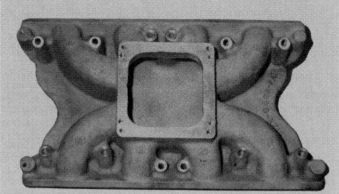

1   2

AK'S ATTACK

when we saw this same engine bolted onto the Heenan-Froude engine dynamometer at the Autolite facility next to Bill Stroppe's shop in Long Beach. Here was the true test. There would be no chance to blame a poor showing on strip conditions, chassis problems, or lack of bite, and we frankly weren't prepared for the results with the same confidence as Ak had. "The dyno neither lies nor forgives," goes an old speed business saying. The Boss 351 proved, though, that no one has to lie about it, putting out an honest 515 hp with one 4-bbl. (a 4500 Holley), and if that wasn't spectacular enough, a full 550 hp with the aid of a Weiand tunnelram with two 660-cfm Holleys! And both of these figures were recorded on straight gas, too. As Ak says, "You can never have *too much* horsepower at Pike's Peak," but this is after all a conservative engine, in that Ak didn't want to exceed 11:1 compression ratio. In fact, Ak said that if the engine was to have been used for drag racing instead of Pike's Peak, the one major difference he would have made would have been to raise the compression to about 13:1. Except for that, the same Ford competition and stock Boss parts would be used for any kind of racing. In the time trials for the Peak, Ak will experiment with several carburetor and manifold combinations, and says he will probably settle on an 800-cfm double-pumper Holley for a good, crisp throttle response.

We didn't have space enough here to go into all the details of the building of this engine, but the most important parts are covered in the accompanying photographs. We have also included several charts, listing the all-important factory part numbers for the "trick" goodies as well as bluprint specs and ignition advance curve data. The data is right from the proverbial horse's mouth and all the more timely, because at press time there has been no book up till now which has covered the Boss 351, although Ford does have a future Muscle Parts Book in the works on this engine. So get your act together and we'll be looking for you out at Pike's Peak, Colorado, on Independence Day to display some Boss Ford fireworks!

IGNITION DATA
(Using kit D1AZ-12A132-A)

Distributor (rpm/spark advance)
200/0°-.5°
400/0°-.5°
500/0°-.75°
600/0°-2°
800/2°-4°
900/4°-6°
1000/8.5°-11° (max)

Point Gap ....18-.22-in.
Initial Engine Timing ...Adjust for 38°-42° total spark advance
Secondary Wires ....Autolite 7SH silicone-covered steel wires
Spark Plugs ....Autolite AF701; AF22 (cold)

351C 4-BBL. BOSS ENGINE BLUEPRINT SPECIFICATIONS

Main Bearings ....Select fit for .0025-.0030-in.
Crankshaft End-Play ....004-.010-in.
Connecting Rod Bearings ....Select fit for .0025-.0030-in.
Connecting Rod End-Play (two rods) .....018-.022-in.
Piston to Bore ....0065-.0075-in.
Piston to Pin ....0006-.0008-in.
Piston Pin to Connecting Rod ....0006-.0012-in. Interference
(pressed pin—minimum 1800 lbs. force to move pin)
Valve Stem to Guide, exhaust ....0011-.0022-in.
Valve Stem to Guide, intake ....0007-.0018-in.
Camshaft Bearing ....001-.006-in.
Camshaft End-Play ....001-.006-in.
Flywheel Hub Face Runout ....002-in.
Damper to Crankshaft ....000-.002-in. Interference
Valve Stem Seal to Valve Stem ....None
(intake and exhaust)
Valve Lash, Intake and Exhaust ....026-.028-in., cold (.025-in. hot)
Piston Ring to Groove ....Compression ring .002-.004-in. Oil Ring snug
Distributor Gear Backlash ....007-.017-in.
Distributor Shaft End-Play ....004-.025-in.
Piston Ring Gap in Bore ....015-.020-in. Compression rings .015-.069-in. Oil ring

351C 4-BBL. "OFF-ROAD" ENGINE COMPONENTS

Part Description	Part No.
1971 Boss 351C Engine Assembly	Code #K-625J
Intake Manifold, 4-bbl. Single Plane	D1ZX-9425-FA
Gasket, Intake Manifold	C9ZZ-9441-A
Gasket, Intake Manifold End Seals	D0AZ-9A424-A1
Gasket, Cylinder Head	D3ZX-6051-AA
Competition Camshaft Kit (Including Lifters)	D1ZX-6250-FA
Intake Valve, Titanium	D0ZX-6507-A
Exhaust Valve, Lightweight	D0ZX-6505-A
Valve Spring Assembly (1.69-in. Installed Height)	D0ZX-6A511-A
Competition Rocker Arm Fulcrum Assembly	D0ZX-6A585-A
Boss 351 Piston (TRW)	D1ZZ-6108-A
Boss 302-351 Oil Pan	D1ZZ-6675-B
Boss Oil Pump	D0AZ-6600-B
Distributor Conversion Kit (Makes stock distributor full centrifugal advance)	D1AZ-12A132-A

3

4

5

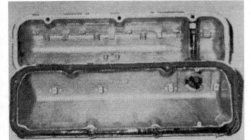

6

7

8

9

1. Steel rocker arms can withstand a lot of high-rpm loads, and the Torrington needle-bearings in the competition fulcrums assure long life.

2. Hot factory manifold for single-4 applications is #D1ZX-9425-FA. Ak cut out the carburetor mounting plate area for more top-end flow. He says some of the newer aftermarket designs in high-rise manifolds work as well.

3. With the valves in the overlap position, the dial indicator is set at 0. Ak slowly turns the rocker arm nut until valve touches piston. If indicator then reads .100-in. or more, your clearance is ok.

4. There are several complicated ways to determine the combustion chamber volume for figuring actual compression ratio. Ak's method is basic and very simple. With the piston at TDC and the valves closed, he fills the hole with automatic trans fluid from this graduated burette. This way includes the piston as well as the combustion chamber in the head.

5. This ISKY "dream wheel" is like a round slide rule. Setting the 351 displacement next to the 8-cylinder mark, we read our volume (71cc) and find that it comes to 11:1, which is just right for Pike's Peak racing. Any more invites overheating at the higher altitudes there.

6. Stock Boss aluminum valve covers are used, but Ak removes the oil drip fingers (as on top valve cover) to clear the polylock rocker nuts used.

7. Once the settings are locked in, a special precaution at the Ak Miller Garage is to dab the screws with 3M Weatherstrip Adhesive so they can't loosen up under racing vibrations.

8. Maximum carburetion for the Boss engine was a tunnel-ram manifold with two 650-cfm Holleys. This Weiand item outperformed similar setups on the Autolite dyno in Long Beach, putting out only 15 hp less than injection!

9. The dyno headers used for tests were 2¼-in. diameter. Note the super deep-sump oil pan here, it's just for extra insurance on the dyno.

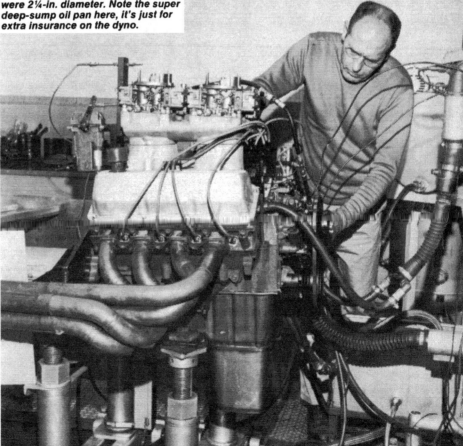

HOW TO PERK UP YOUR 351C

With budgets of $100, $250 and $500, you can brew up a really potent 351C

Of the engines we'll discuss, the majority of them (roughly seven out of every ten) were two-barrel-carbureted versions rated at 250 hp, while the remaining thirty percent carried four-barrel carburetion and a horsepower rating of 300. Because there are numerous differences in the heads, valvetrains and inductions systems between the two-barrel and four-barrel versions, our recommendations will be tailored specifically to each of these versions, as applicable. Our overall goal will be to approach the performance offered by the BOSS 351C engine, using Ford parts.

In most cases aftermarket equipment can be substituted, but since Ford is our source of information, we'll keep it all Henry. Much of the information that follows has been extracted from Ford's Off Highway Parts Book. You can get a copy of this book, which covers all Ford engines, by sending $1.50 to: Off Highway Parts Book, Milwaukee Junction, P.O. Box 5386, Detroit, Michigan 48211. It's a good investment.

The 351C responds very favorably to carburetion changes, so if you're on a limited budget, that's the place to start. If you're starting with a two-barrel engine, you'll need to change

By C. J. Baker ■ Last month we told you how to pump more power from 289- and 302-cubic-inch Ford V8s. This month we'll climb up a notch in displacement to Ford's popular 351 Cleveland engines and explore their performance potential with budgets of $100, $250 and $500. Approximately one million of these 351Cs have been produced, but due to federal emission laws restricting the alteration of 1970 and newer engines used on public roads or highways, we'll concern ourselves with the modification of those engines built before 1970. This doesn't mean that 1970 and newer 351Cs and 400Cs are to be avoided. These same modifications will work on these later engines, but it is only legal to so modify them if they are used for strictly off-highway purposes. The truth is that some of the '70 and '71 351Cs are real stormers just the way they came from the factory, especially the '71 BOSS 351C.

intake manifolds. The cheapest way to do this is to find a four-barrel manifold from an early 351C (the later ones are drilled for spread-bore carbs) in the salvage yard. The used manifold should sell for about $20. It is important that you pick a manifold that is designed for a standard-flange carburetor; that is, one that has similar-sized primary and secondary bores as compared to the spread-bore carbs that have small primaries and huge secondary bores, since we will be recommending a standard-flange four-barrel carburetor. If you can't find a used manifold, your local Ford dealer will be happy to sell you a new one (part No. D0AZ-9424-C) for $47.95.

If you already have a four-barrel manifold or if you want something better than the stock cast-iron unit, Ford does offer an aluminum hi-rise intake manifold (part No. D1ZZ-9424-G), which sells for $96. Many good aftermarket aluminum manifolds also fall into this price range, so the choice is yours. Regardless of whether you choose the cast-iron or the aluminum manifold, install it using the Boss 302 paper intake manifold gaskets (part No. D1ZZ-9433-A), selling for $2.95, to assure proper sealing.

Admittedly, the purchase of an aluminum manifold just about wipes out our $100 budget, but there is still some hope in the carburetor department. For most mildly modified street-driven 351Cs, the 735-cfm carb (part No. C9AZ-9510-N), listing for $65.25, is the hot tip. However, this is the same carburetor that was standard equipment on the 428-cubic-inch CJ engine, so with a little luck you'll be able to find one in a salvage yard for $15-$25. If you buy a used carburetor, it's always a good idea to pick up an inexpensive carb rebuild kit and restore the unit to like-new shape before installing it (see "Rebuild Your Carb for $5," October '72 HRM).

If you buy an aluminum manifold and a new carb, the tab could run as high as $170, but if you're starting with a four-barrel engine and shopping in the salvage yard for the more desirable 735-cfm four-barrel carb, while retaining the original manifold, $20 might be enough to complete the above modifications. The result is up to 35 hp added to the two-barrel engine and 11 hp to the four-barrel version. Depending on where you fall in this money picture, you might also want to add the 360-degree-inlet chromed air cleaner (part No. C5ZZ-9600-W), but it'll cost you another $30.75.

$250

If you can afford to spend a total of $250 on your 351C, the next steps, in addition to the changes already mentioned, will be to improve the valvetrain and the ignition system. These changes will include a high-performance cam and valve springs, plus upgrading the distributor to dual points.

Regardless of whether you're starting with an engine that was originally equipped with a two-barrel or a four-barrel carburetor, the cam to get is the high-performance hydraulic version (part No. D1ZZ-6250-A), which sells for $36.25. The stock hydraulic lifters can be retained if they are in good shape, but new valve springs (part No. C90Z-6513-E) are required to handle the higher lift of the new cam. A complete set of springs will run $22.26.

The stock rocker arms, pushrods, retainers and keepers are all usable, but if you're starting with a 351C that originally had a two-barrel carb, it will also be necessary to replace the rocker arm fulcrums. The stock fulcrums are aluminum on these engines and they won't stand any sustained high-speed operation with the hotter cam. The fulcrums to get are the sintered-iron versions (part No. D00Z-6A528-A) that were used on all four-barrel 351Cs. These sell for $17.60 a set.

In the ignition department, the changes you'll have to make

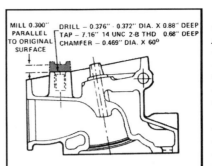

LEFT—Modifying the four-barrel cylinder heads for a solid-lifter valvetrain requires milling the rocker stud pedestals as shown.
BELOW—Four-barrel, Boss and CJ heads feature much larger ports than the two-barrel versions.

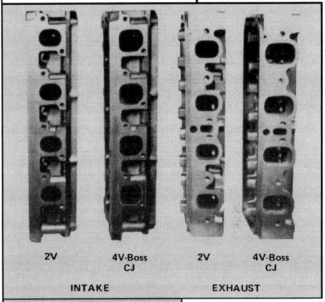

2V	4V-Boss CJ	2V	4V-Boss CJ
INTAKE		EXHAUST	

LEFT—Degreeing the camshaft for peak performance is simple with this crankshaft timing chain gear (part No. D1ZX-6306-BA).
BELOW—Upgrading to dual points requires nothing more than a conversion kit for stick-shift cars. Automatics must use a dual-diaphragm distributor to achieve a livable idle with a hot cam.

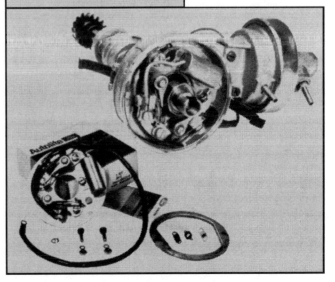

351C

depend on whether your car is equipped with a manual transmission or an automatic. If it's a manual, all you need to pick up is the dual-point-conversion distributor kit (part No. D1AZ-12A132-A), selling for $13.20. This kit contains a new breaker plate, spacer, new points, condensor and assorted springs, along with detailed instructions for modifying your distributor.

If you have an automatic transmission, you'll need to replace the stock distributor with the '71 Boss 351C unit. This dual-point distributor employs dual vacuum diaphragms, which are necessary to get the engine to idle at a speed that is slow enough to be compatible with the automatic trans. This distributor sells for $30.40 and is listed under part No. D1ZZ-12127-D. Install the unit with a single manifold vacuum line to the diaphragm farthest from the distributor housing. To time the engine, disconnect and plug the vacuum line and set the initial timing at 16 degrees BTDC. Reconnect the vacuum line and set the idle speed at 700 rpm in gear.

Depending on whether you started with a two-barrel or a four-barrel, an automatic or a manual trans, whether you opted for the aluminum intake manifold and whether or not you engaged in junkyard shopping, you might have enough of your $250 left to buy a set of aftermarket headers. All of these mods will boost the horsepower output of the basic two-barrel engine to approximately 325, while the four-barrel 351C will climb to roughly 365 hp. The reason that the basic four-barrel engine will produce 40 more horsepower is due to the design of the combustion chambers and the larger port size that was not incorporated on the standard two-barrel heads.

$500

If you're bucks up and really want a strong-running 351C, there are a number of modifications that can be made to a standard two-barrel or four-barrel Cleveland that will boost its output to over 400 hp. In essence, these changes upgrade these engines to the configuration of the Boss 351C. So before you start to buy parts, the best plan of action is to attempt to locate a used '71 Boss 351C. Although they are fairly rare, chances are that $350 or $450 will buy one of these hot performers, and you'll still have your stock 351C to sell for $250 or $300, providing it's in good shape. In this way, you might be able to move up to the Boss 351C for as little as $50. Not only is this the cheapest and easiest way to go, you'll also gain such things as four-bolt main bearing caps and the high-compression pistons that aren't included in our $500 hop-up budget. For off-road use, the only things you'd want to change on the Boss engine are the aluminum intake manifold and the spread-bore carburetor, and even the ones that come on the Boss 351C are desirable enough to have good resale value. The combination you'd want to swap to would be the aluminum hi-rise manifold (part No. D1ZZ-9424-G) or an aftermarket version and an 850-cfm Holley R-4781-AAS carb. These parts will run about $200 if purchased new.

If you can't locate a '71 Boss 351C and you decide to modify your existing 351C (providing you've got at least $500 to spend), the parts and procedures you must use depend on whether you're starting with a two-barrel- or a four-barrel-carbureted 351C. We'll begin with the two-barrel version.

In this section we'll assume that you're starting with a standard engine and that you haven't performed any of the modifications previously mentioned in the $100 or $250 sections. Start by getting a four-barrel carb. Either a 780-cfm or an 850-cfm

unit will be suitable, with the 850 version being the most desirable. Ford lists three different versions of the 780-cfm carb. The first is part No. D00Z-9510-N, which is for manual-transmission cars with an automatic choke. The second is part No. D00Z-9510-R, for automatic-transmission cars with an automatic choke. The third unit is part No. D00Z-9510-Z, for stick-shift cars, and it features a manual choke. Any of these three 780 carbs can be purchased for $80.95. If you decide to use an 850-cfm carb, select the Holley R-4781-AAS double-pumper unit. Since this is a non-Ford part, you'll have to go to an aftermarket supplier to get this one.

To mount the carb, the ideal manifold to use is the aluminum hi-rise unit (part No. D1ZZ-9424-G), selling for $96. An aftermarket aluminum manifold will also do the job here if you'd rather go that route. If you can't afford an aluminum manifold, use the cast-iron version (part No. D0AZ-9424-C), selling new for $47.95 or used in a salvage yard for about $20. If you do use the cast-iron manifold, it will be necessary to open up the manifold throttle bores to a diameter of 1.75 inches to prevent carburetor throttle plate interference when the 780- or 850-cfm carbs are used. Either way, use the intake manifold gasket kit (part No. D0AZ-9433-A), which lists for $6.75.

For adequate ignition at high rpm, a dual-point distributor is mandatory. For automatic-transmission cars, order the complete dual-diaphragm distributor (part No. D1ZZ-12127-D), which sells for $30.40. Install this unit as described in the $250 section. If the car has a manual transmission, the $13.20 dual-point-conversion kit (part No. D1AZ-12A132-A) is all that's required to upgrade the stock distributor.

Cylinder heads are the next area of concern. Pick up a pair of the Boss 351C heads (part No. D1ZZ-6049-B), which will cost $134.10. In addition to the bare heads, you'll need the following coordinated parts.

Part:	Number:	Price:
Intake Valves	D0ZZ-6507-A	$34.80
Exhaust Valves	D0ZZ-6505-A	43.60
Keepers	C9ZZ-6518-A	4.29
Valve Springs	D0ZZ-6513-A	17.48

Valve Spring Seats	D00Z-6A536-A	8.24
Retainers	C9ZZ-6514-A	5.28
Sintered-Iron Fulcrums	C9ZZ-6A528-A	1.98
Rocker Arm Studs	C9ZZ-6A527-A	9.40
Rocker Arm Stud Nuts	C8ZZ-6A529-B	10.40
Guide Plates	C9ZZ-6A564-A	3.72
Pushrods	D00Z-6565-F	25.60
Rocker Arms	C9ZZ-6564-A	26.40
Camshaft (mechanical)	D1ZZ-6250-B	39.10
Lifters (solid)	D0ZZ-6500-A	29.60
Head Gaskets	D0AZ-6051-C	6.10

The above parts will complete the cylinder head assemblies and the high-performance solid-lifter valvetrain. Because of the high-rpm capability of this cam and valvetrain, the following parts should also be replaced in the bottom end: connecting rod bearings (part No. D1ZZ-6211-A), listing at $10.88; main bearings (part No. D1ZZ-6333-A) at $7.44; and the main thrust bearing (part No. D1ZZ-6337-A), which sells for $4.37. While you're replacing the bearing inserts, install the good 180,000 psi rod bolts (part No. D1ZZ-6214-A), which will cost you $4.80, and the rod bolt nuts (part No. D1ZZ-6212-A) that sell for $2.48.

This completes the changes necessary to upgrade the two-barrel 351C to a real performer. If you have a manual trans and you manage to find a used cast-iron intake manifold and a used carb, this hop-up can be accomplished for approximately $500. However, if you're running an automatic and you purchase a new aluminum manifold and a new carb, the tab could climb as high as $642. Of course headers and a good performance ring and pinion gear will also help performance, but since we've exhausted our budget, you might try getting these items by writing to: S. Claus, c/o North Pole.

Now we're ready to attack the four-barrel 351Cs. Actually, many of the parts required for the four-barrel version are the same as those required for the two-barrel engine. Of course the four-barrel motor will already be equipped with the cast-iron intake manifold which can be retained if it is reworked as outlined in the two-barrel section. Carburetor selection, intake manifold gaskets and distributor modifications are also identical to the two-barrel.

The major difference in this section is that the cylinder heads on the four-barrel 351C can be reworked to be compatible with the solid-lifter valvetrain, as these heads already have the same larger ports and open combustion chambers that are featured on the Boss heads. To rework the heads, it will be necessary to mill .30-inch from each slotted rocker arm stud pedestal. It is important that the pedestal be milled parallel to the bottom of the slot and not parallel to the bottom of the head. This is true because each pedestal is set at a compound angle to achieve the "canted valve" configuration of the 351C. After the pedestals are milled, they must be drilled and tapped as shown in the accompanying diagram to accept the rocker arm studs (part No. C9ZZ-6A527-A), which sell for $9.40.

The rocker arm stud nuts, valves, keepers, fulcrums, guide plates, pushrods, cam, lifters and head gaskets are all identical to those listed for the two-barrel modification. However, the stock retainers and rocker arms from the original heads can be retained if they are in good shape. There is also a different valve spring required for this setup (part No. C90Z-6513-E). These springs sell for $22.26. Valve spring seats are not required with these valve springs. The same bearing and connecting rod bolt changes that were made on the two-barrel should also be made on the four-barrel engine.

Because new cylinder heads aren't required for the four-barrel engine, $350 should be enough to complete the modifications if the car has a manual transmission and the cast-iron manifold is retained in conjunction with a used carb. That leaves $150 for headers and gears. If the car has an automatic trans, and an aluminum manifold and a new carb are purchased, the total will climb to just over $500. In this case, headers and gears once again find themselves on the Christmas "wish" list.

This wraps up our study of the 351C. These motors are capable of some real neck-snapping power, but you have to dig a little (especially into your pocket) to get it. Next month we'll inspect the 390- and 428-cubic-inchers. Who says we don't write stories for Ford lovers! ▪▪

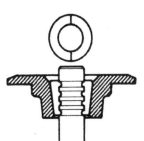

Multi-Groove
Promotes valve rotation on 351C 4V & CJ engines

Single-Groove
Gap between keeper halves promotes tight grip on 351 Boss engines. Also used on 302 Boss.

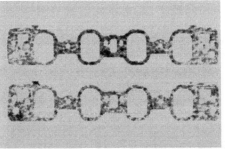

LEFT—When installing a four-barrel manifold on a two-barrel engine, the Boss 302 paper gaskets should be used to assure proper sealing. BELOW—Modifying the two-barrel 351C requires the expenditure of a lot of money, but up to 400 hp can be obtained with stock parts.

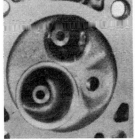
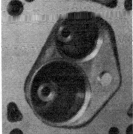

Open   Quench

ABOVE LEFT—The four-barrel 351C is a better hop-up choice, since both the stock intake manifold and heads are adequate for good breathing. LEFT—Premium bearings are a must for high-rpm reliability. ABOVE—Two-barrel 351Cs used a lower-compression open combustion chamber. Four-barrels used the tighter quench chamber.

Bud Moore's
NASCAR "Mini-Motor"

Building a Boss 351 Ford, Southern style

BY JAY STORER

hen a name like Bud Moore Engineering has been around the racing game for so many years and won countless races in both NASCAR and SCCA Trans-Am competition, it's hard to think of him as ever being considered an underdog, yet this is exactly how the railbirds are looking at Bud's latest Grand National stock car effort. Grand National stock car racing is traditionally "big" racing; the cars are full-size, the engines are the biggest and most potent semi-stock versions the factories have got, and it takes big men to drive these cars at up to 200 mph, bumper-to-bumper. So when one of the biggest names in GN car building, Bud Moore Engineering, announces it intends to mix it up with the big boys with a "little" Ford 351 engine, it's bound to set people talking, and knowing BME's reputation for winning, this is one small-block that

engine enthusiasts everywhere will want to take a closer look at.

Given the requirements of pushing a 3800-lb. car around a high-banked oval track at high speeds and high rpm for hours at a time, why would anyone want to do it with a comparatively small engine? Scoffers have referred to the BME 351 as a "mini-motor" and to its GN challenge as a "David vs. Goliath" confrontation, but when there's an expert like Bud Moore behind it, you can't discount the idea that perhaps he's going to scoop everyone with a better slingshot.

Moore began working seriously with the Cleveland 351 last year as an alternative to the bigger engines of GN racing. Armed with years of experience in developing high-performance parts for Ford (when they were racing), especially during the years when BME campaigned the winning Trans-Am

Mustangs of Parnelli Jones and George Follmer, there were more than a few reasons for switching to the smaller motor in the GN cars.

One is cost. Grand National stock car racing is really expensive. A good GN car easily costs what the finest Pro Stock drag machine costs, and you need two or three cars to put out a worthwhile effort, one for the big tracks, one for the short tracks, and one as a spare. Then, on top of all of this, you've got to have spare engines, chassis pieces, and a gaggle of tires and wheels. Then you need a highly-trained, efficient pit crew who know every nut and bolt in your car, and naturally you need a top driver to get anywhere. This adds up to a sizable investment even if you're factory-backed. Now that (as of Feb. 6) Ford has dropped completely out of the racing picture and the other manufactur-

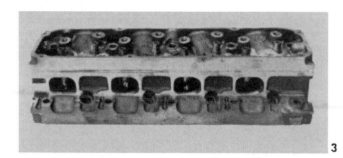

36

ers are also cutting back to spend more money on solving emissions and safety problems, the cost of racing is going to be even higher for the car owner. One answer to this could be the smaller engines.

HOW STOCK IS STOCK?

Since even the *name* of the type of racing implies that the cars bear some

1. *Streaking around NASCAR's big ovals is second nature to a pro like Bobby Isaac, but even a pro needs a good mount to win. Well, they don't come much better built than a Gran Torino 351 by Bud Moore Engineering.*

2. *Awaiting delivery to a customer, here's a Boss 351 for NASCAR's Late-Model Sportsman racing. It's been built, dyno'ed, partially torn down for checkout, and reassembled ready to drop in a car and race. Let's follow a Grand-National engine as it's built, starting with the BME high-exhaust-port Cleveland heads.*

3. *The BME high-port heads begin life as a stock Boss 351 head, from which the upper, outer half of the exhaust side is machined away.*

4. *The aluminum plate that makes up the new exhaust side of the head requires extensive machining. Here's a plate attached to the cut head before the port has been raised.*

5. *Scribe marks are made for the new higher port when the aluminum plate is bolted on the head. Then the plate is removed so the new port can be cut on the Bridgeport mill.*

6. *When the ports in the head and plate match, the plate can then be machined until it's parallel to the head on all the outside surfaces.*

7. *To strengthen the head and avoid gasket problems, special studs are run through the rocker arm stud holes (arrows). These go all the way down and bottom out inside the water jacket, shoring up potential weak areas on the engine block side.*

8. *After machine work is completed on a set of high-port heads, porting and polishing of the combustion chambers is the next process, and it's a tedious, hand-labor job.*

9. *Compared to the stock head at left, the finished racing head at right will flow better, cc more easily, has no hot spots, and makes power!*

10. *After his brother Ken has done the "P&P" number on a set of heads, Steve Blackwell checks out each port on the flow bench. If it doesn't flow to BME specs, more grinding is done until it's absolutely perfect.*

11. *Steve also does the cc'ing and head assembly work. It took 68.4 cc of fluid to fill a chamber on this head, necessitating a slight milling job on the head for correct compression.*

12. *Before assembly, the heads are cut for Perfect-Circle valve seals, but only on the intake guides.*

6

8

10

11

7

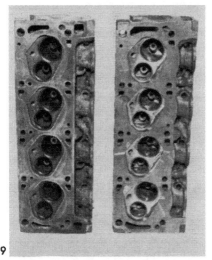

9

12

"Mini-Motor"

resemblance to what you can buy at your local dealership, so-called product identification *should* be a feature of GN racing, but up until now the serious efforts have been with exotic, big-inch engines not generally available to the public. In fact, most of the current GN engines being used, such as the 426 Hemi Chrysler, 427 Ford, and 429 semi-hemi Ford, aren't even manufactured anymore, and builders have resorted to the aftermarket for exotic pieces to keep them in the running. In fact, the competitive builders have come up with enough "secrets" to make the big engines run faster now than before NASCAR made them put restrictor plates or "thimbles" under the carburetors to keep the speeds down and make for closer competition.

Believing, as Bill Jenkins does, in the possibly higher efficiency of smaller engines, Bud Moore expects to challenge the big motors in '73 with his white 351 Gran Torino cars, sponsored by Sta-Power engine conditioners. Besides building and maintaining their own race cars, the business at BME is building racing engines for stock cars, drag machines and sports cars. Most of the highly-respected engines go to racers in NASCAR's competitive Late-Model Sportsman division. A combination of factors points to the desirability of the small-block motors for GN rac-

ing: BME's heavy business in building 351 Sportsman engines, the desire to race what they sell, the better product identification of running an engine the factory makes in quantity for the public rather than special one-off motors, plus the efficiency of the smaller motors and the fact that they can run without restrictor plates (NASCAR plates or thimbles are required only on engines over 366 cu. in.). Bud Moore feels this is just the beginning of the "mini-motor" era for NASCAR, and that it will be better for all concerned: racers, manufacturers, and spectaters.

Our entry into the Bud Moore shop (some 14,000 sq. ft. of racing activity) was a rare privilege, for this is the first printed look-see into the inside of one of his Grand National engines. The more you see of the assembly of one of these engines, the more you realize that most of the innards *really are* stock Ford high-performance pieces, with the racer's edge in this case being the careful, precision assembly—true blueprinting. So much time is involved in preparing the pieces for assembly that a racing engine usually takes over a week to be completed. After only a short time at BME, you get an overwhelming impression of the *organization* of the shop. With all the engines that pass through their doors, they have to be organized. Working under shop foreman Ken Myler is a dedicated crew of professionals, each man with a

specific job to do. The visitor passes from the machine shop area through the engine assembly room, the balancing and head assembly room, and on to the two dyno rooms where all engines are tested. It's a complete facility where nothing is ever "sent out," the kind of facility every hot rodder dreams about.

"HI-PORT" HEADS

Probably the most interesting part of the Bud Moore engines are the "hi-port" heads, which resulted from BME's development program for Ford high-perf pieces. Basically, the heads are milled so that one whole corner of the head (upper exhaust side) is removed lengthwise. Then an aluminum plate is machined to fit the head in this area, the pieces are bolted together and ported and polished to match each other. This is oversimplifying, because the whole process takes some 34 man-hours to complete. What this trick does is heighten the angle of the exhaust ports for better flow. The ports on the Boss 351 Cleveland heads are big, and the head breathes well with the canted valve arrangement. However, the exhaust ports come out of the combustion chamber and right away have to make a 90° turn to get out to the exhaust headers. By using the high-port plates, the angle is reduced to 45° when the port is raised, which effectively straightens out the port and

1

2

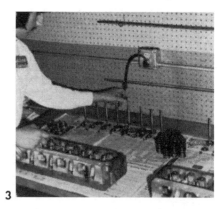

3

4

5

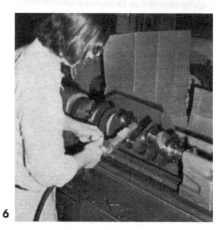

6

pumps another 20 good horsepower into a racing engine. You've probably seen such modified heads on the top Ford Pro Stockers at the drags, as Gapp and Roush also make this modification. The accompanying photos should clarify exactly how the aluminum plates are made to fit and how they raise the angle of the ports.

After the heads are machined and fitted with the plates, they become the responsibility of Steve Blackwell and his brother Ken, who together do the rest of the headwork at BME. Ken does the basic hard work of porting and polishing the ports and combustion

chambers, and then Steve flow tests every port on each head to make sure they meet BME specs. Every customer receives a numbered and matched set of heads modified to the same specs as those on Bud Moore's own Bobby Isaac-driven GN car.

Most of the racers who buy BME engines return there for any later work or rebuilding, and the original specs can be brought out for comparison. After flowing the heads, Steve then checks the combustion chamber volumes by cc'ing and determines how much the heads have to be milled to come up with the optimum chamber

volume for the compression ratio desired. Generally, only one chamber need be measured with the burette and liquid, since Steve has found that after the chambers have been polished there's seldom a variance of more than .1 cc between chambers on the same head.

With the heads cc'd and milled, Steve turns his attention to fitting the valves and assembling the valve train. The valves used are stock Boss 351 items, Part No. DOZX-6505-A for the lightweight, 1.71-in. exhaust valve and Part No. DOZX-6507-A for the titanium intake valve. Since the exhaust

1. The Rimac spring tester tells Steve whether the Ford 3-piece valve springs meet the 120 lbs. spec at the proper installed height.

2. Using a snap gauge to measure from the spring seat (allowing .080-in. for the spring seat bucket) to the retainer for each valve, Steve selects the proper spring shims.

3. Everything at BME is done in a clean, organized manner. Steve oils the heads and puts all the correct shims in place in preparation for installing the springs and valves.

4. With the spring seat buckets and shims in place, the PC seals are slipped on the intake guides and crimped with the PC tool (foreground).

5. Valve train components for the BME Boss 351 consist of Ford 3-piece springs, Crane aluminum roller rockers, and lightweight Ford racing valves. At lower right the valve spring seat "buckets" (arrows) are visible.

6. Buddy Hawkins prepares a Boss 351 crank by grinding off all the parting lines and sharp corners on the counterweights, where stress cracks can start. Except for this polishing and balancing, the cast (nodular iron) cranks are run stock.

7. Crank balancing done the old way, without the heavy mallory metal, often meant drilling and filling with five or six plugs. Using mallory metal (only two or three plugs) saves time.

8. The crank is first pre-balanced with extra weight, then balanced with the dampener and the flywheel.

9. The 351 engine used a heavier counterweight on the dampener; this is why extra weight is added to the crank itself when BME utilizes the lighter 302 pulley, gear and plate.

10. Note also the difference in the counterweights used on the flywheels. The nodular iron 302 flywheel can be obtained now through BME.

11. Absolutely the first thing done to connecting rods is to number the rod and its mated cap as soon as they come out of their Ford box.

12. If there's a burr on the bearing locater slot, it could raise that area of a bearing and cause failure, so the sharp edges are filed.

7

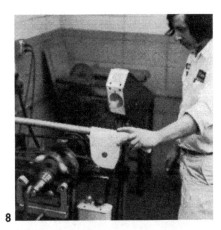

8

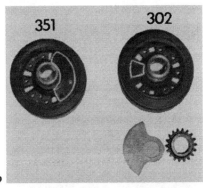

9

351   302

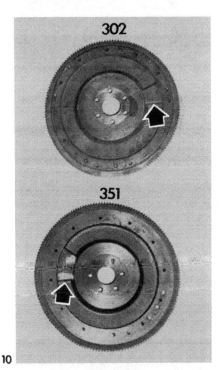

302

351

10

11

12

"Mini-Motor"

valve is .035-in. larger than a stock valve, the first cut Steve makes is with a reamer, to bring the holes to the right size. Both intake and exhaust seats are cut with three angles, 60°, 45° and 30°. Seat widths are .080-in. for the exhausts coupled with a .060-in. intake seat on a GN engine. For a drag racing engine the seat widths would be reduced to .060-in. on the exhausts, and Steve said the intakes would be *thin!*

Valve springs (Ford triple spring Part No. DOZX-6A511-A) are selected to come up with a set that make 120 lbs. on the spring tester at 1.83-in. installed height. The Ford spring seat "buckets" that sit on the head take up .080-in. Thin shims are used to make

up for variances in spring seats to make them all the same height between the spring seat and the bottom of the retainer. Actually, the springs used in the first assembly of a new engine are only 80-90 lbs. strong. These are used for dyno testing the engine and give the cam a chance to break in without wearing round. After the testing on the dyno, the stronger "race" springs are installed and the engine thoroughly checked out before sending it to the customer.

SHORT-BLOCK PIECES

Naturally, the block used for all the 351-in. BME engines is the Part No. D1ZZ-6010-D, Boss block with 4-bolt mains and "selected hardness" main caps, used with the Part No. D1ZZ-6303-A crank, which is special nodular iron. Yes, it's a cast crank, but

perfectly suitable for racing use. In fact, it's the same crank used in the Pro Pintos of Dyno Don and others, because a forged steel crank isn't available for this engine. The Moore team hasn't experienced any crank trouble, even running at 7200 rpm for 500 miles of GN racing. Buddy Hawkins is the short-block components preparation man at BME and does all the engine balancing work. The Boss crank is left pretty much stock, except that a special hand-held belt sander is used to grind off the casting flash and remove any sharp edges on the counterweights that might be stress points.

The small-block family of Ford engines use an "external" balance from the factory, which means that some of the weight used to balance the crank is designed into both the front dampener and the flywheel. What Buddy

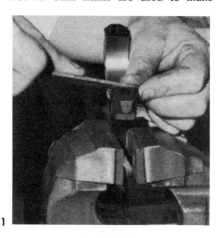

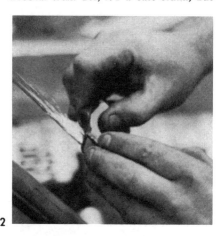

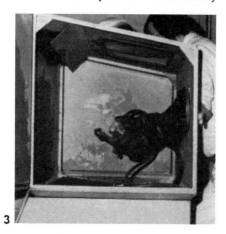

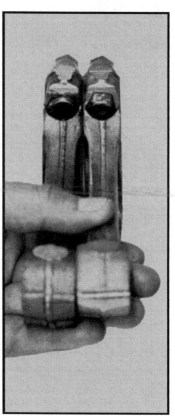

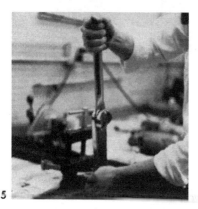

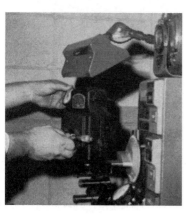

does to modify this is to use the lighter 302 dampener and flywheel, then add weight to the crank itself during what he calls "pre-balancing." Normally this is done by drilling out sections of the crank counter-weights and welding in blobs of metal that are heavier than the metal removed in drilling the holes. The metal used at BME is called "mallory metal" and is 2½ times as heavy as lead. Using the mallory metal instead of normal crank balancing material saves three hours in pre-balancing alone.

When Buddy is satisfied with the pre-balance, he attaches the 302 dampener and flywheel and balances the total package. The flywheel used at BME is the 10½-in. nodular iron unit developed for the Boss 302, and this particular unit is now available only from BME, which purchased all the

finished and unfinished ones from Ford.

Although they have toyed with aftermarket specialty connecting rods, BME uses regular, off-the-shelf Boss 351 rods in both customer engines and their own GN motors. You can't go into a 500-mile race with any variables or parts you're not quite sure of, and they know they can trust a blueprinted Ford rod. Rods, like other internal engine parts, are either magnafluxed or Zyglo-inspected before selection, just for insurance sake. The rods (Part No. D1ZZ-6200-A) are then shot-peened for strength. Buddy doesn't feel it's necessary to grind the sides of the rod beams down flat, preferring instead to "polish" the high spots on a fine-grit belt sander to remove stress points along the beam and around the big end.

Precision equipment is in evidence everywhere you look at BME, and particularly where any of the internal engine components are concerned. A cut of .0015-in. is taken off the mating face of each rod and its cap, so they can then be bolted together and sized on the Sunnen rod-reconditioning machine. With the cap torqued on, both ends of the rods are honed to precisely the size desired. Incidentally, the standard rod bolts are replaced with Ford competition-type bolts (Part No. D1ZZ-6214-A, 4 pcs.) and nuts (Part No. D1ZZ-6212-A, 8 pcs.), which are still ⅜-in. in diameter but strong enough for any kind of racing use.

Including the balancing stage, in which all the rod big ends are balanced and then the total rod weights made the same, six man-hours are spent in blueprinting a set of eight

1. Rubber vise jaws protect the rod while sharp edges are filed.

2. Both the rod and its cap are next "polished" on a fine-grit belt sander to remove sharp edges, especially along the beam and rod bolt areas.

3. Although the end door would of course be closed during any normal operation, this is what the inside of a shot-peening booth is like.

4. The stock bolt on the rod at left has a football-shaped head, different from the racing bolt (right).

5. After taking .0015-in. off the rod and its cap, they are held in a special vise and torqued together.

6. It never hurts to double check when you're dealing with blueprint work, so Buddy checks the gauge on Sunnen rod reconditioner with a mike.

7. After the rods are "undercut," they are put on the gauge of the rod reconditioning machine in order to check the size of the big-end bore.

8. The machine is used to precisely hone the rod's bore to the desired "blueprint" size. A good job means proceeding a little at a time and always rechecking on the bore gauge.

9. All weights and measures of the engine's internal components are carefully recorded for future reference. Here the sides of the big-end are measured to determine rod side play.

10. Buddy uses the Shadowgraph to balance the rod big-ends first, then to get all rods to the same weight.

11. The TRW pop-up pistons require only a slight facing for more intake valve clearance (arrow).

12. Any sharp edges on the pistons are also removed or filed down, in this case to prevent any scratching on the cylinder walls.

13. The pin bore of every piston is measured on the Sunnen machine, and they are honed just as the rods are to come up with the right size.

8

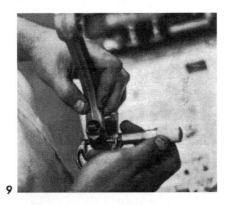

9

10

11

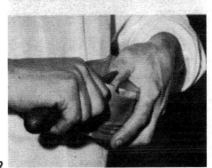

12

13

"Mini-Motor"

rods. It's this kind of attention to detail that wins races and keeps engines together.

Special TRW-made pistons (Part No. L-2348-F) are used in the GN engines, as you can't get more than about 11.3:1 compression with stock Ford Boss 351 pistons. The TRW's are a pop-up design not unlike the Ford units, but feature 12:1 compression when used with the proper heads. The 1971 351 Boss heads had a quench-type combustion chamber, which is necessary to get this high compression (in fact, the TRW pistons were designed to go with the 1971 heads). Boss 351 heads in 1972 had open chambers (no quench area) because they produced lower emissions, so the earlier heads are preferred if you want high

compression for racing. The only modifications to the pistons are oil holes added to the pin bosses and a *slight* extra cut made for intake valve clearance on the head of the piston. All the machined edges of the pistons are smoothed out with emery cloth, and the pistons are balanced with their pins.

Assembly of the pistons to the rods is interesting. Instead of *pressing* the pin through, the rod's little end is heated in a small, precise oven for one minute. This expands the little end enough for Buddy to quickly push the pin through the piston and rod by hand. This way there's no chance of the pin cocking or galling going through the rod, as could conceiveably happen if it were forced in cold with a press. The pins used are not original types, but the Part No. C9ZZ-6135-E replacement items.

ASSEMBLY

While all the internal engine parts are being prepared as described above, the block itself is also being blueprinted. Decking, precision honing, boring, etc. are all within the realm of a shop equipped as completely as BME. After all the surfaces of the engine have been squared away, the 4-bolt main caps are torqued down with new bearings in place so that all the clearances can be checked. As you might expect, the engine assembly room (for that matter, each of the work areas at BME) is kept super-sanitary.

Supervising the assembly room is ace mechanic "Ducky" Newman, and Bud Moore's young son Daryl also does assembly work, dividing his time between this room and running engines in the shop's two dyno rooms.

The bearings are precisely measured

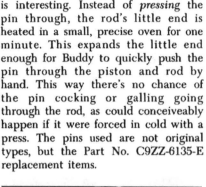

1

2

3

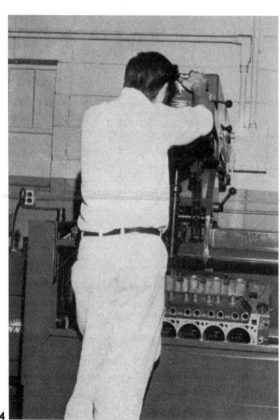

4

5

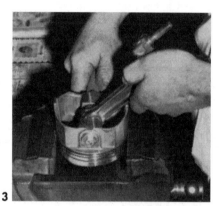

6

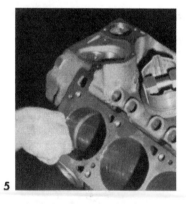

7

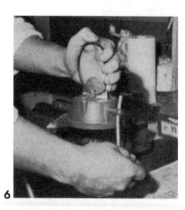

8

42

while torqued in place on the block, and comparing this measurement with a miking of the crank's main journals gives the clearance. All the bearings in the shop are miked and marked for identification, so that a set of bearings can be select-fitted to a particular engine. In the same manner, rod bearings are measured while torqued in the rods and select-fitted to come up with the desired clearance. Main and rod clearances used are .0025-.0030-in., with the sides of the rod big-ends ground to provide .022-.025-in. clearance between rods on the same crank journal. Once the block has been honed to provide .0065-.0075-in. clearance between the pistons and the cylinders, attention is focused on the rings. Rings to fit the custom TRW pistons are available from RAMCO or Perfect Circle. Ducky uses a piston to square the rings in a cylinder so that the ring end gaps can

be measured. If they don't come out wide enough, he grinds them slightly in a fixture made specifically for the purpose until the desired .015-.020-in. end gap is obtained (gap is .015-.069-in. for the oil rings).

Installing the rods and pistons in the engine with the blueprinted and balanced crank in place is pretty straightforward, with lengths of rubber hose slipped over the rod bolts to avoid nicking the crank journals. Factory specs are used in torquing down the 4-bolt mains and rods: 95-105 ft-lbs. on the ½-in. bolts, 35-45 ft.-lbs. on the ⅜-in. main bolts, and 45-50 ft.-lbs. on the connecting rod nuts (oil under the nuts). Everything going into a new engine is thoroughly lubricated either with engine oil or Ford engine oil conditioner. The all-out competition cam used is Ford's .600-in. lift, 320° duration model (Part No. D1ZX-6250-FA),

which comes with special lifters ground on a radius to match this cam. The stock timing chain and gears are utilized, and even the stock nylon-toothed cam gear has been found to be reliable at high rpm.

There are two basic ways to go with the oiling on the Boss 351: dry or wet sump. The BME team uses a special dry sump pump driven by a small chain from a thin gear on the crank (behind the dampener). All the bolts on the oil pump are safety-wired together to prevent loosening under racing's vibrations. The system is topped off with a custom windage tray and a long, low cast-aluminum oil pan. This is what they use on their own GN engines, but it's an expensive setup, so most customers opt for a stock Boss 351 oil pump, for which Ford offers an optional relief spring (Part No. D2ZX-6670-A) for 100 psi oil pressure

1. Pins are very difficult to balance by themselves, because it's hard to remove or add weight to them, so they're balanced with their pistons.

2. Instead of press-fitting the rod to the piston and pin, the rod's little end is heated in this oven, which expands the hole for the fitting.

3. The heated end is expanded just long enough for Buddy to insert the pin with a special holding tool.

4. Ducky Newman runs the Cylinder King for a perfect honing pattern on the Boss 351's cylinder walls.

5. After the head of a piston has been used to square up a ring in the block, Ducky checks the amount of the ring's end gap with a feeler gauge.

6. The desired .015-.020-in. gap is quickly obtained on this filing fixture, which keeps the ends square.

7. As with all the other steps in building a racing engine, when it comes time to fit bearings, precision instruments are used and all specs are recorded for future reference.

8. A micrometer is used to double check the accuracy of the tool used to measure the engine's mains

9. With the bearings in place and the 4-bolt mains torqued in place, Buddy sizes the bores, which, when compared to the crank measurements, tells him what the clearances are.

10. With all the clearance work and bearing selction done, everything can now be lubricated and assembled.

11. These special radiused lifters must be used with (and only with) the hot Ford OHO mechanical cam.

12. The pan BME sells for stock car racing is this deepened version of the stock Boss oil pan.

13. The BME and stock Boss pans both feature built-in windage trays to keep the oil around the pickup.

9

10

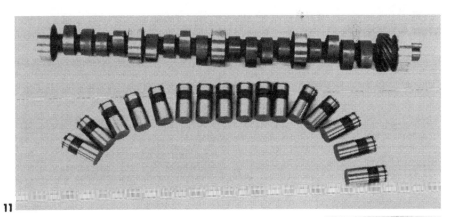
11

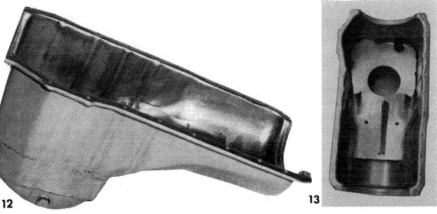
12   13

"Mini-Motor"

with this pump, and a BME deep-sump pan. The deep pan is based on the stock Boss pan, which has a built-in windage tray. BME also offers a road-racing pan with trick trap-door baffling. The road-racing pan gets its additional oil capacity from widening rather than deepening so that more ground clearance can be provided for low-down racin'.

TOPSIDE ASSEMBLY

Once the bottom end has been buttoned up, the engine is turned right-side up on the engine stand and the above-deck components installed. It was found while racing the Boss 302's in Trans-Am that the small-block Ford was prone to blowing head gaskets, so this led Ford and BME to develop a heavy-duty model. This gasket, Part No. D3ZZ-6051-A, is available from Ford and should take care of head sealing problems for any normally-aspirated engine. The BME high-port heads are bolted in place and torqued down, in sequence, at 15 ft.-lb. increments from 60 ft.lbs. to the final 120 ft.-lbs. (125 ft.-lbs. hot). The heads are fitted with stock Ford screw-in rocker arm studs (Part No. C9ZZ-6A527-A), pushrod guide plates (Part No. C9ZZ-6A564-A), and Crane aluminum roller-tip rocker arms. The rocker arms are one of the few aftermarket pieces used.

Sitting up on top of the engine for all to see, the induction system comes in for more than its share of attention from most engine fans. The choice is fairly wide for the Boss 351, depending on the application and the budget. For the low-budget approach, the Ford single-plane, high-rise aluminum manifold (Part No. D1ZX-9425-FA) works well for high-rpm power, but Bud Moore has done a lot of development work with small-block Fords and has come up with his own manifold, called the Bud Moore "Mini-Box." It's a single-plane, plenum-type manifold with a removable cover. Not only can internal changes be made to suit any purpose, but different covers can also be used for different carburetion.

This manifold was developed for the 302 engine, and since the 351 has a wider block, a precise block and head spacer must be used between the engine and the BME Mini-Box. A spacer like this is no job for an amateur to machine (BME's machinists spend 16 man-hours on each spacer plate), as you can tell by the photographs of it. A spacer is usually sold with every BME manifold, since the Mini-Box is what most of the customers order. A new manifold of similar design, to be called the "Maxi-Box," is in the works

(a prototype of it is on the BME race cars) and may be in production by the time you read this story. It will be made to bolt directly to the wide Cleveland block without a spacer plate.

Ignition on the BME Grand National engines is the high-dollar Ford transistor system, but shop foreman Ken Myler says a properly set up stock distributor with the dual-point kit (Part No. D1AZ-12A132-A) should also be up to the task. Distributors are curved on a Sun machine to come up with 8°-11° in the distributor. Enough is run on the crank for a total of 38°-40°

One of the lasting impressions one takes away from a visit to BME is the thorough, professional way they approach everything. All the way through the building of an engine, whether for their own cars or for a customer, all the minute data are recorded—headwork, balancing, bearing-fitting, etc. In fact, there's nothing left to memory; a complete "medical history" is available for any engine that goes out the door, not the least of which is the final dyno report.

Two complete dyno rooms make up part of the BME facility, and every engine is run and tested on "the wheel" before delivery. Not only does this insure that the engine is indeed operating at peak efficiency, but it gives all the new parts a chance to break in under controlled conditions. Before running an engine for the first time, not only is an electric drill attachment inserted into the distributor hole to spin the oil pump for insured initial lubrication, but space heaters are used in the dyno rooms to pre-heat the oil pan so that engines start right out on warmed oil.

At the time of our visit to BME, the engine we photographed during its progress was finally put on the big Henan-Froude dyno (known in the shop as "Bud's Toy"). There it sang out with a sweet and honest 515 horses, with the single-Holley-equipped Maxi-Box. Out on the high-banked oval tracks, that engine will deliver its power for 500 miles at around 7200 rpm. Try that with a lot of engines (remember, this Boss 351 uses mostly stock parts) and you'd be spinning around in your own oil so fast you wouldn't know which way to the pits. Winning is closely tied to *survival* when you're talking about GN stock car racing; you've got to make power, but you have to make power *live*, too. So when you drop a BME-built Boss 351 Ford into the honed-to-perfection racing chassis hiding under the white Gran Torino body of the number 15 Sta-Power car and add a veteran wheelman like Bobby Isaac...you've got a slingshot designed to take on the big-block giants.

1. A dry sump oiling system, which requires this special long windage tray, is used on the BME GN engines.

2. After the cam and timing gears are in place, Ducky installs the thin gear that drives the internal pump for the Grand National oil system.

3. For safety's sake, all the bolts that have to do with the oil pump are safety-wired together.

4. With the pickup bolted and safety-wired in place, Ducky then bolts up the water pump and the front cover.

5. The special cast-aluminum pan that is part of the dry sump system not only bolts to the block, but is also held to the front cover by 11 bolts.

6. Some of the external parts of the dry sump are shown here. The aluminum fan pulley's second V-belt drives the idler pulley, which drives the Gilmer belt for the external pump.

7. The resistor block and amplifier assembly for the Ford transistor ignition are mounted inside the race car to protect them from engine heat.

8. The BME Mini-Box intake manifold was originally designed for the 302. Hot setup is with the cover made for a single Holley 4-bbl. carburetor.

9. A total of 18 hours of machine work goes into making one of these spacer plates to adapt the 302-type manifold to the 351's wider block.

10. Daryl Moore watches as his famous father loads the engine on his big Henan-Froude dynomometer. Every BME engine is checked out here.

11. After a dyno run, engines are partially disassembled so that the heads can be retorqued and the innards checked out. Daryl uses a probe light here to check the cam wear.

12. After a hot lap on the "wheel," the old master himself stands back to admire his handiwork, while Daryl and Steve reset the valves. Equipped with prototype Maxi-Box and a 4500 Holley, the mostly-stock-equipped Boss 351 Ford made 515 honest horses.

8

9

10

11

12

CLEVELAND CONFIDENTIAL

TOP SECRET

Overlooked by most racers, Ford's 351C is a real off-the-shelf eye-opener

LEFT — 351 Cleveland engines in the four basic configurations: A. 2-barrel; B. 4-barrel; C. Cobra Jet; D. HO or Boss 351. OPPOSITE PAGE, ABOVE LEFT — The 351 Cleveland block has an integral front housing for the water pump, thermostat, fuel pump and direct water passage to the cylinder heads. ABOVE RIGHT — Valves set at compound angles give the 351 heads their designation "canted valve." BELOW LEFT — Cylinder head on the left used the early "quench" combustion chamber. Later head on the right uses larger "open chamber." BELOW RIGHT — From left to right, early flat-top piston had 10.7:1 compression ratio, while domed version featured 11.1:1 for high-performance engines. '72 flat-top piston has only 9.2:1 squeeze.

By C. J. Baker ■ It seems that in the world of high-performance engines, the 351 Cleveland has been one of the best-kept secrets in recent years. The 351 Cleveland is one of those series of outstanding performance engines that has apparently been overlooked by most hot rodders. Of course, not all versions of the 351C are suitable for competition usage — Ford has to build some for little old ladies too. But Ford does produce two versions that are real stormers: the 351C-CJ and the super-strong 351C-HO (sometimes called the Boss 351).

Before we go into a detailed examination of the CJ and HO engines, we'll review briefly the design basics of the 351C series. The 351C block is unique from other Ford small-blocks in that it includes an integral cast housing for the water pump, thermostat and fuel pump. This housing also incorporates water passages which facilitate the circulation of water directly to the cylinder heads without going through the intake manifold, providing a faster warm-up without hot spots. Eliminating water passages from the intake manifold also permits the design of more efficient manifold runners.

All of the 1972 351C blocks which were to receive a four-barrel carburetor were equipped with four-bolt main bearing caps, as were the '71 CJ and HO engines. All other 351s have two-bolt caps. However, all 351C blocks are cast with extra-wide cap-to-block mating surfaces to accept four-bolt main bearing caps. Therefore, blocks with two-bolt caps can be updated to the four-bolt caps. Since the four-bolt caps are not sold separately, they must be obtained from a discarded block or machined from 1010 steel.

The last major design feature of the Cleveland engines is the use of canted-valve cylinder heads. Canting the valves toward the ports allows another port design and provides optimum flow characteristics. This design produces a more efficient flow pattern by reducing the sharpness of the port turns that are normally required with vertical valve replacement. The ports follow a nearly straight line to the valve centerlines; thus, a more uniform cross-sectional area can be used than is possible with rectangular ports. (See illustration.)

Now that we've acquainted you with the basics of the 351C's design, we'll enlighten you about the component variations between the 351C Cobra Jet engine, called the CJ, and the Boss 351C-HO, called the HO (high output). We will exclude the standard four-barrel 351Cs built up to 1972, and all the two-barrel versions, as they are not generally considered high-performance engines. In 1972 the four-barrel 351C and

the 351C-CJ are identical, so we'll just refer to them both as the CJ.

Perhaps the most significant difference between the CJ and the HO engines is that the CJ uses a hydraulic-lifter camshaft and associated valve train while the HO uses mechanical lifters. The type of valve train used dictates several other component changes between the two engine versions. The CJ, with its hydraulic lifters, utilizes a positive-stop rocker arm arrangement with cylindrical-type fulcrums seated on individually slotted pads. A fulcrum guide is milled in the cylinder head pedestal for each of the independently mounted stamped rocker arms to position and lock the mating fulcrum guide. The cylindrical T-shaped fulcrum and rocker arms are bolted to the pedestal to provide a positive-stop feature which requires no adjustment. A more positive control of the rocker-arm-to-valve-tip re-

lationship is attained by locking the fulcrum in the milled slot on the pedestal with a 5/16-inch bolt, thus improving durability of the valve tip and assuring high-speed valve train stability.

The HO, with its mechanical lifters, requires a provision for valve lash adjustment. To facilitate this, the rocker arm stud pedestals on the HO heads are machined flat instead of with the milled slot that the CJ and all other 351C heads received. In place of the T-shaped fulcrum, the HO gets a fully adjustable cylindrical fulcrum mounted on a 7/16-inch stud. Rocker-arm-to-valve-tip relationship is maintained by using pushrod guide plates in this system. For additional durability, the HO gets specially hardened and ground pushrods, stamped steel valve spring seats, higher pressure valve springs, single-groove tight-gripping valve keepers, and short-skirt valve seals for improved lubrication.

The valve sizes on the CJ and the HO are identical, with 2.19-inch intakes and 1.71-inch exhausts. There is, however, some variance in the combustion chamber design between the two engines in different years. The '71 CJ, '72 CJ and the '72 HO heads are identical, featuring "open" combustion chamber configurations of 7.39 to 76.9cc. However, the '71 HO employed a "quench" combustion chamber configuration of 64.6 to 67.6cc. This change on the '72 HO, along with changes in piston dome configuration, was made to make the engine compliant with '72 emission requirements.

Four different types of pistons have been used in '71 and '72 CJ and HO engines. In 1971 the CJ used a cast-aluminum, flat-top piston with a compression ration of 10.7:1. In 1972 the same style of piston was used, but the compression ratio was dropped to 9.0:1. Unlike all other 351Cs, the HO uses a

47

CLEVELAND

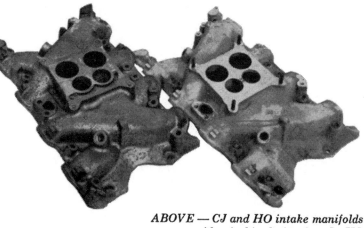

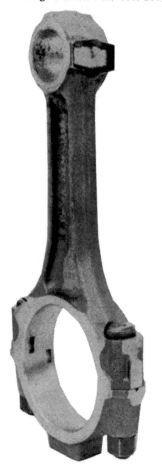

BELOW — Connecting rods for both the CJ (left) and the HO (right) are forged 1041-H steel, but HO rod is shot-peened and magnafluxed. HO rod also gets a more durable 180,000-psi bolt.

ABOVE — CJ and HO intake manifolds are identical in design, but the HO unit is cast from aluminum (right) while the CJ receives cast iron.

ABOVE — Harmonic dampers vary in weight for different engine applications. 2V and 4V engines get the lightest unit, while the CJ receives the middleweight. The heavy damper is reserved for the HO.

forged-aluminum piston. In 1971, the HO piston featured a pop-up dome for a compression ratio of 11.1:1. This was a very good piston, and a compression ratio of 12.0:1 could easily be obtained by reducing deck height and milling the heads. In 1972 the pop-up dome was replaced by a flat-top on the forged piston for a compression ratio of 9.2:1. This change makes the '71 engine a better choice for any serious competition usage.

The connecting rods for both the CJ and the HO engines are forged from 1041-H steel, but the HO units are shot-peened and magnafluxed. In addition, the HO rods get a more durable ⅜-inch, 180,000-psi bolt in place of the ⅜-inch, 150,000-psi bolt used in the CJ rod. Incidentally, the HO rod bolts will fit in any of the other 351C rods. This would be a wise swap when doing an engine overhaul.

A cast-iron crankshaft is used in both engines, although the HO gets a crank

selected for hardness (90% nodularity). The lubrication system for both engines is identical; however, the dipstick on the HO engine is recalibrated for a six-quart oil fill instead of the five-quart oil fill used for other 351Cs. Running that sixth quart of oil is another good idea to employ on all 351Cs.

Different harmonic dampers are also used on the various Cleveland engines. The CJ gets a damper that is slightly heavier than the standard production 2V and 4V dampers, while the HO gets a still heavier damper designed for high-rpm operation. (See photo.)

On top of the engine, identically designed intake manifolds are used on both the CJ and the HO engines. The only difference is that the HO manifold is cast from aluminum while the CJ's is cast-iron. Use of the HO manifold on the CJ is a great weight-saving tip.

Carburetion on both the CJ and the HO engines is handled by Autolite

4300-D spread-bore carburetors, varying only in calibration. Ignition chores are handled by dual-point, dual-diaphragm distributors, again varying only in calibration.

One final distinction given the HO is the use of cast-aluminum valve covers, while all other 351Cs get stamped steel covers.

As we said at the beginning, the 351C seems to have been overlooked, but we hope to remedy that. While in Detroit, we had an opportunity to drive a Mustang with the 351C-HO engine. The performance and tractability of the HO was impressive — doubly so when we found out that the Mustang weighed 3750 pounds. It was enough to make us wonder what the HO would be capable of if it received the full treatment and was installed in a lightweight body. The truth is, we're thinking seriously about doing it ourselves for a future story!

■■

FIRST AID FOR A BLEEDER

Text & photos by C.J. Baker ■ There's one common stumbling block associated with the modification of most engines for racing use: They were originally designed as passenger car engines and not racing engines. Consequently, it is not uncommon to find parts or systems that worked satisfactorily on the street that are totally inadequate or unacceptable on the race track. A good example of this is the Ford 351C oiling system.

The stock 351C oil system pushes oil from the pump to the front main bearing and into two lifter galleries along either side of the camshaft. Then, after feeding the lifters, and all of the upper valvetrain, whatever volume of oil is left in these galleries flows to the main bearings and through the crankshaft to the rod bearings. The cam bearings are also fed off the main bearings.

There are two distinct flaws in this design. First, a large amount of oil volume and pressure is bled off the system at the lifters before the mains are lubricated. Comparatively, lubrication of the valvetrain has a much lower priority than lubrication of the mains. And second, if a component should fail in the valvetrain, such as a rocker arm or a pushrod, which would allow one of the lifters to pop out of its bore, all oil pressure would be lost to the mains. Since such a failure would probably happen at high engine speed, the engine would, in all likelihood, be destroyed.

Now there's a way to modify the 351C oiling system to eliminate these problems. The fix was originally developed at Hank the Crank's shop in North Hollywood, California, to solve the lubrication problems being encountered by NASCAR mechanics as they switched to the small-block engines to comply with the latest rules. However, this fix will work equally well on any 351C competition engine, whether it's for a boat, drag racing or circle track use.

The basic concept of Hank's system is to provide separate and direct lubrication to the main bearings, which still supply

Getting adequate oil to the 351C main bearings has always been a problem, since the oil system loses both performance and flow at every place possible on its way to the crank. Here's the latest solution

ABOVE—Moroso junction block serves to divide the oil flow between the rear main and left lifter gallery (lower 3/8-inch line) and the center three main bearings (upper 1/2-inch line).

both the rod and cam bearings, while restricting oil flow to the valvetrain to the minimum required for safe operation. To do this, a Ford Econoline van oil filter adapter is modified so that 1/2-inch-i.d. braided-steel line supplies oil directly from the pump to a junction block at the rear of the block. At this point, the oil is split into two lines, one a 3/8-inch-i.d. line that feeds the rear main bearing and also the left lifter gallery through a .060-inch restricter orifice, and a 1/2-inch-i.d. line that supplies an oil manifold fabricated in the lifter gallery just above the camshaft. This manifold feeds oil to the center three main bearings. The front main is still supplied by the stock internal

oil passage which runs directly from the oil pump. Oil also flows from this front passage through a .060-inch restricter orifice to feed the right lifter gallery.

Naturally, to accomplish all of this, oil passages must be drilled to the center three main bearings, the original oil passages to the two lifters galleries must be closed off, and all the proper restricter orifices must be installed. The result is oil delivered directly to each main through a 5/16-inch orifice, and each lifter gallery is supplied through a .060-inch orifice. If a valvetrain component fails, oil can only bleed off from the system through one of the .060-inch openings, so the mains are still assured of adequate lubrication. Study the photos and you'll get the idea as to how all of this is accomplished. If you're thinking of building an all-out 351C, get in touch with Hank. It could save you a lot of headaches in the long run. ■■

ABOVE—This is the C5TE-6884-A Econoline oil filter adapter that is modified to supply oil to the rear of the block through the 1/2-inch braided steel line.

BELOW LEFT—A separate oil manifold is fabricated to carry the oil from the 1/2-inch line and distribute it to the center three mains through specially drilled and restricted passages. BELOW RIGHT—Oil arrives at the mains through a 5/16-inch passage (arrow 1), where it flows through an opening in the main bearing, not shown, and also behind the main bearing to a .040-inch restricter orifice (arrow 2) on its way to the cam bearings. The rear main has an additional .060-inch restricter orifice (arrow 3) that supplies oil to the left lifter gallery.

FORD, MERCURY "CLEVELAND" V-8

351 and 400 Cubic Inches • 163 to 255 Horsepower

GENERAL/Last year Ford offered four separate variations of its 351 2-bbl. Cleveland engine, plus an additional two versions of the 351 4-bbl. (Cobra Jet). Also, there were three different bhp-rated versions of the 400-cu.-in. Cleveland (which comes only as a 2-bbl.). This year there is no such variety—just a single engine in each category (see chart). However, at the time of writing, Ford hadn't yet set its bhp and torque figures for the California-only engines; so, there will doubtless be other ratings besides those which appear on the accompanying chart. (California horsepower/torque figures should, of course, be expected to be lower than those listed here, due to that state's tougher emissions regulations.) In '74, all Cleveland engines destined for sale in California will come with a solid-state ignition system; for this reason, plug gaps now have a revised setting of .054-in. It should also be noted that the 351 Cobra Jet is not available at all in California.

Ford introduced the 351-cu.-in. "Cleveland" in 1970 as the newest entry in its lineup of small-block V-8's. In those days it sported compression ratios ranging from 9.0:1 all the way up to 11.0:1. However, as everyone knows, things have changed in the last few years as Detroit has adjusted its engines to run on regular fuels. The 351-cu.-in. and 400-cu.-in. Cleveland engines now come in just two compression ratios: 7.9:1 for the 351CJ, and 8.0:1 for the others.

Although the Cleveland and the 351 Windsor engines have the same displacements, bore and stroke, and center-to-center bore spacing, (4.38 ins.), they are in many ways very different powerplants. Physically, the 351C has a bit longer block, its front being extended about 2 ins. in order to encompass the timing chain and its gears. This has the advantage of allowing a flat stamping to cover the timing mechanism, thus eliminating the need for a complex (and expensive) casting. What really sets the Cleveland apart from the Windsor, though, is its use of canted valves. This permits a more efficient intake port design and at the same time allows the use of bigger valves, since the valves are able to open and close in an overlapping pattern rather than parallel to each other. It's important to note that the Cleveland heads are not interchangeable among the heads used on any of Ford's other small-block V-8's, because of a redesign of the water passages from

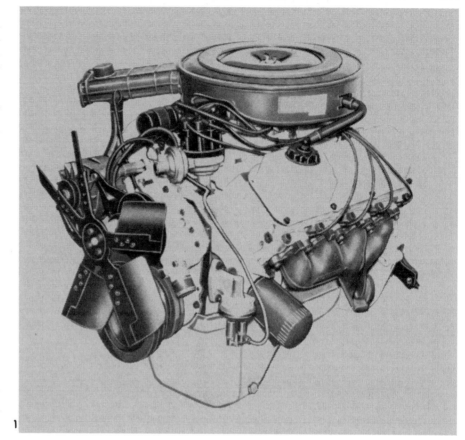

1

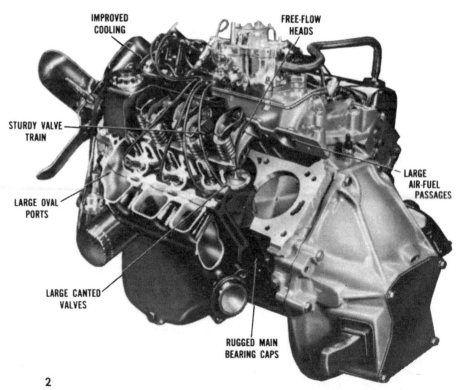

IMPROVED COOLING

FREE-FLOW HEADS

STURDY VALVE TRAIN

LARGE OVAL PORTS

LARGE AIR-FUEL PASSAGES

LARGE CANTED VALVES

RUGGED MAIN BEARING CAPS

2

1. *Exterior of Cleveland Small V-8 reveals nothing unusual. Most of the differences from the Windsor engines are internal ones.*

2. *In cutaway, the staggered and canted valves show; they are the single major difference in the newer Cleveland powerplant.*

3. *Positions of rocker arms and pushrods also differentiate the Cleveland.*

4. *Valve guides in Cleveland head are angled rather than parallel.*

shares the canted valves of the 351C, but uses longer connecting rods and larger piston pins and has a taller block deck-height.

There are no longer any real high-performance engines left in the Cleveland series—not since the end of the '71 model year when all such engines were phased out and compression ratios sliced to the bone. However, the Cleveland does have the distinction of being the base unit for the last true hi-po engine to come off the FoMoCo line—the 351C HO 4-bbl. of 1971. This was the engine which replaced the 302 HO (as found in Boss Mustangs) as Ford's hot setup. The 351C HO carried with it innumerable high-performance components right off the showroom floor. Standard items included such things as a 750-cfm Autolite carburetor, high-lift cam with mechanical lifters, high-domed extruded aluminum pistons, magnafluxed connecting rods, and special-tolerance cranks with 4-bolt caps. At 11.0:1, the compression ratio wasn't exactly anemic either. But that was 1971—this is 1974. If you want a 351C HO now, you'll have to study the used car ads in your local newspaper very carefully (or get lucky at a junkyard).

For quick engine identification, check the Safety Certification Decal mounted on the left front door-lock face panel. This decal bears the Vehicle Identification Number, the fifth character of which identifies the engine by cubic-inch displacement and carburetor type (see chart). An identification tag is also affixed to the engine itself and indicates the displacement, model year and month of production of the engine. (On the Cleveland engines, this tag is located under the ignition coil bracket.) The Vehicle Identification Number (this is the official title and registration number) is also stamped on a metal tab fastened to the dash close to the windshield on the driver's side and is visible from the outside.

PISTONS/All of the Cleveland series engines use steel-strutted cast aluminum alloy pistons. They're all slipper-skirted, "cam ground," and tin-plated, and all have two compression rings and one oil control ring. No. 1 compression is barrel-faced cast iron alloy with a molybdenum-filled groove. The lower compression is taper-faced cast iron alloy, has a scraper groove and is phosphate-coated. The oil ring is multi-piece, with two rails and a spacer-expander. Rails are SAE 1070 steel, chrome-plated and black-oxide coated, with the spacer-expander being rustless steel (SAE 30201). Piston pins are heat-treated SAE 5015 steel and are a press-fit in the rod. The connecting rods are SAE 1041-H forged steel

the block on the Cleveland. Last year the 351C also became available as a 351CJ. These two engines are basically similar except that the CJ's use a 4-bbl. carburetor and have a little bit stronger bottom end.

The other version of the Cleveland is a 400-cu.-in. powerplant which was produced (in 1971) by a ½-in. stroke increase over the 351C. (The 400C is perfectly "square," having a bore and stroke of 4.00x4.00 ins.) The 400C

"CLEVELAND" V-8

and have replaceable, plated copper-lead alloy steel-backed inserts. Con rod center-to-center length on the 351's is 5.78 ins., while on the 400 it's 6.58 ins. The numbers on connecting rods and their bearing caps must be on the same side when the assemblies are installed in the cylinder bore. Additionally, pistons should always be fitted with the arrow on the dome facing the front of the engine.

CRANKSHAFT/Also common to all Cleveland engines is a 5-main-bearing, precision-molded, nodular cast iron alloy crank. The 351C 2-bbl. uses steel-backed lead-base babbitt bearing inserts, while the 351CJ uses plated copper-lead alloy on steel backs. Bearings on the 400 are the same as those on the CJ, except that they are unplated. End-thrust is taken by No. 3 main bearing, and end-play is .004-in. to .008-in. The Cobra Jet engine uses 4-bolt main bearing caps, as did the now defunct 351C HO; all other Cleveland engines use the more conventional 2-bolt caps. Main bearing caps are selective fits, and they should never be filed or lapped or fitted with bearing shims to obtain the correct clearance.

CAMSHAFT/The chain-driven camshaft on all Cleveland engines is a special alloy cast iron unit and is precision-molded, induction-hardened, and phosphate-coated. It runs in five lead-base babbitt, steel-backed replaceable inserts. The camshaft sprocket has a die cast aluminum body and molded nylon teeth.

VALVES/The main difference between the Windsor and Cleveland engines is in their valves—the canted arrangement of the latter allowing for the use of bigger intakes as well as exhausts. Intakes on the 351W are 1.843 ins.; exhausts are 1.541 ins. All the Cleveland engines (including the Cobra Jet) use 2.041-in. intakes and 1.654-in. exhausts. Valve material is slightly different among the three Clevelands: The 351C 2-bbl. and the 400C use SAE 1047 steel and an aluminized head, while the 351CJ 4-bbl. has valves of No. 1 Sil-chrome with chrome-plated stems and aluminized head. Exhausts are 21-4N steel with aluminized heads; however, the exhausts on the Cobra Jet are also chrome-plated. Hydraulic lifters are standard and no valve rotators are used. Lifter units are matched assemblies and internal parts should not be interchanged.

LUBRICATION/The rotor-type pump is located inside the crankcase and supplies oil to the system at a pressure of 50 to 70 psi at 2000 engine rpm. The main bearings, con rods, cam bearings, and lifters are all lubricated under full pump pressure. Piston pins on the 351C 2-bbl. and 4-bbl. are oiled by a timed pressure stream. The 400's pins are lubricated by oil mist and splash. Timing gear on both 351's gets metered pressure, while the 400's timing gear gets a directed spray. Cylinder walls are lubricated by metered

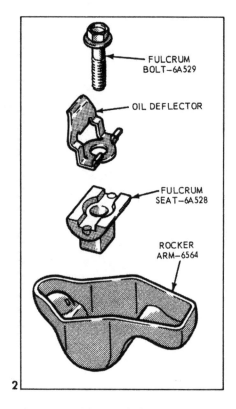

FULCRUM BOLT—6A529

OIL DEFLECTOR

FULCRUM SEAT—6A528

ROCKER ARM—6564

2

1. When installing split, lip-type rear main oil seal, face lip to front of engine. Don't apply sealer to area forward of oil slinger groove.

2. Cleveland V-8's use stud-mounted rocker arms, have integral oil deflector. Be sure fulcrum seat base is fully seated in its slot on cylinder head before tightening bolts.

3. Cleveland V-8's use single retainer, compared to 2-piece retainer of small V-8's. Note damper is fitted to 351-cu.-in. Cleveland only.

4. Camshaft is induction-hardened, has phosphate coating. Note 2-piece fuel pump eccentric.

5. Connecting rods and bearing caps are numbered on all Cleveland engines. Numbers must be on same side when assemblies are fitted to cylinder bores. Arrow on piston top should face front of engine.

6, 7. The Cleveland series engines all have efficient, rounded intake ports (top) and exhaust ports in their heads.

8. The 351C HO "Boss" engine (right) was a high-performance version and is no longer available as an option. (It was dropped after '71.) From bottom of block, the most obvious virtue is use of 4-bolt bearing caps.

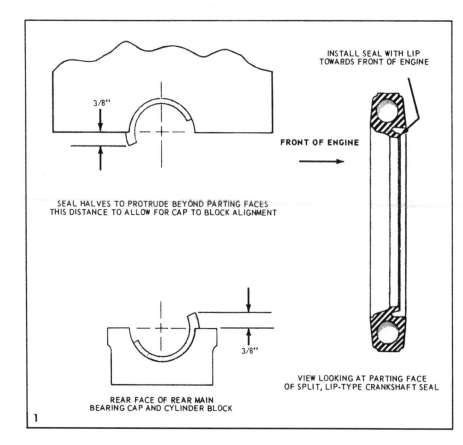

3/8"

SEAL HALVES TO PROTRUDE BEYOND PARTING FACES THIS DISTANCE TO ALLOW FOR CAP TO BLOCK ALIGNMENT

REAR FACE OF REAR MAIN BEARING CAP AND CYLINDER BLOCK

3/8"

INSTALL SEAL WITH LIP TOWARDS FRONT OF ENGINE

FRONT OF ENGINE

VIEW LOOKING AT PARTING FACE OF SPLIT, LIP-TYPE CRANKSHAFT SEAL

1

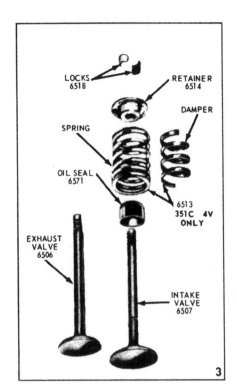

LOCKS 6518

RETAINER 6514

DAMPER

SPRING

OIL SEAL 6571

6513 351C 4V ONLY

EXHAUST VALVE 6506

INTAKE VALVE 6507

3

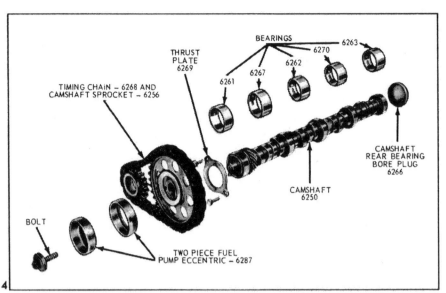

TIMING CHAIN — 6268 AND CAMSHAFT SPROCKET — 6256

THRUST PLATE 6269

BEARINGS

6270   6263

6261   6267   6262

CAMSHAFT REAR BEARING BORE PLUG 6266

CAMSHAFT 6250

BOLT

TWO PIECE FUEL PUMP ECCENTRIC — 6287

4

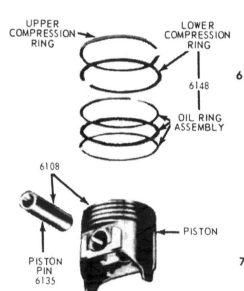

6

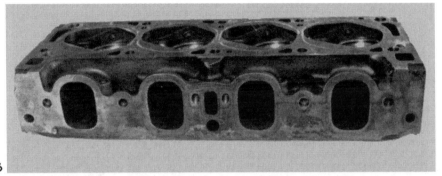

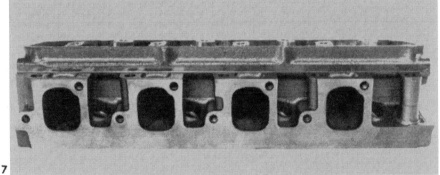

7

UPPER COMPRESSION RING

LOWER COMPRESSION RING

6148

OIL RING ASSEMBLY

6108

PISTON

PISTON PIN 6135

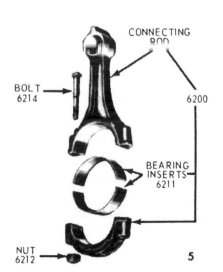

CONNECTING ROD

BOLT 6214

6200

BEARING INSERTS 6211

NUT 6212

5

8

53

"CLEVELAND" V-8

stream on the 400C and a combination of oil mist, spray, and splash on the 351C and 351CJ. All of the Cleveland engines have a crankcase capacity of 4 qts., with an extra quart going into the filter.

FUEL SYSTEM/The Cleveland engines all use a single Ford/Rawsonville carburetor. The 2-bbl. versions have a throat diameter of 1.689 ins. while the 4-bbl. has 1.565-in. primaries and 1.690-in. secondaries. All are, of course, designed to operate on leaded or unleaded fuels with a Research Octane Number of 91 or above. The mechanical fuel pump is located on the left side of the engine and operates at a pressure range of 5.5 to 6.5 psi. Filters are the standard saran plastic at the tank and nylon/monel cloth at the carburetor fuel line.

1. Oil pump on Cleveland engines is Ford rotor-type. When assembling, make certain identification dimple on outer race faces outward on same side as dimple on rotor.

2. Tighten intake manifold bolts on 351C and 400C in sequence shown, 5/16-in. bolts to 21-25 lbs.-ft. and ⅜-in. bolts to 27-33 lbs.-ft.

3. Cleveland head bolts are tightened in order shown and in steps, first to 55 lbs.-ft., then 75, then 95-105.

4. Cleveland engines may use either of two different hydraulic lifter assemblies. "Type I" (top) has a metering valve to determine leak-down rate (oil flow through lifter). "Type II" has no valve—leak-down rate depending on internal clearance between plunger and tappet body.

5. Current Cleveland V-8 uses 2-bolt main bearing caps. Oil pickup (left) is directly connected to oil pump.

6. Exploded view of Cleveland crankshaft shows all related bolts and parts. Cleveland crank is cast iron. Cobra Jet engine is only Cleveland still using 4-bolt main bearing caps, like those used on old 351 Boss.

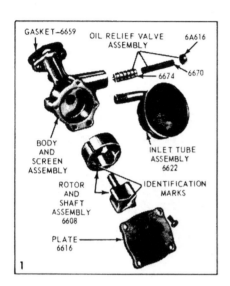

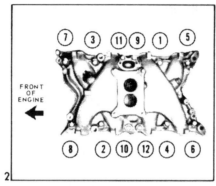

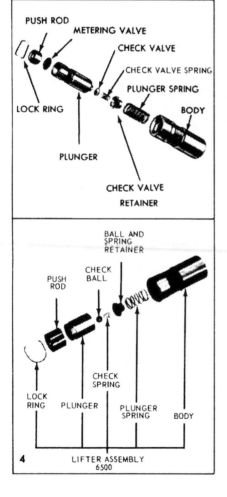

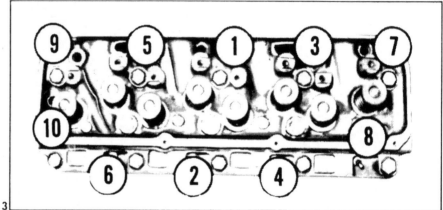

FORD, MERCURY "CLEVELAND" V-8	351C/163 V-8	351CJ/255 V-8	400/170 V-8
Displacement (cu. ins.)	351	351	400
Horsepower @ rpm	163 @ 4200	255 @ 5600	170 @ 3400
Horsepower per cu. in.	.464	.721	.425
Torque (lbs.-ft.) @ rpm	278 @ 2000	290 @ 3400	330 @ 2000
Bore (ins.)	4.002	4.002	4.00
Stroke (ins.)	3.500	3.500	4.00
Compression Ratio	8.0:1	7.9:1	8.0:1
Carburetion	2-bbl.	4-bbl.	2-bbl.
1974 Engine Code	H	Q	S
Length/Width/ Height (ins.)	28/21/22	28/21/22	28/21/22

5

FLYWHEEL

CLUTCH PILOT BUSHING

MAIN BEARING INSERTS

CRANKSHAFT

CRANKSHAFT SPROCKET

KEY

FRONT OIL SLINGER

MAIN BEARING
INSERTS

WASHER

DAMPER

PULLEY

MAIN BEARING
CAPS

BOLT

6

Here's how we go about building a stormin' Cleveland

By Jack Roush

PROFECTING
THE 351C ... for the street

In May we discussed modification of the 289- and 302-cubic-inch small-block Ford V8s. This month we'll turn our attention to the 351 Cleveland V8. As before, we'll try to use Ford parts wherever possible, unless there's a need for an aftermarket substitute to gain reliability or performance. In essence, we'll be building the equivalent of a 9.2:1 compression ratio BOSS 351C with a power output of approximately 400 hp.

Virtually any 351C block can be used, since there are no differences in materials or strength. In fact, the two-bolt main cap block (part No. D0AZ-6010-C) is just as good as the four-bolt main block (part No. D1ZZ-6010-D). Even the caps seem to be equivalent in strength. So unless you already have a four-bolt block, don't spend the extra bucks for this feature.

The only special work required on the block is a thorough removal of casting flash and careful radiusing of the No. 2 and No. 4 main bearing saddles and webs to reduce the likelihood of cracking. During sustained high-speed operation, virtually every 351C block will eventually crack in these areas. Gapp & Roush does offer two

different heavy-duty blocks with thicker cylinder walls and support in the main web area for such applications, but they're not really needed on the street.

Although much has been said about the supposedly poor oiling system in the 351C, it is really quite adequate for high-performance use. Simply install the Moroso No. 2205 kit that restricts oil to the rear four cam bearings and the left lifter gallery. That's all I do to our Pro Stock engines, and we've never seen any oiling problem. Even the stock oil pump is acceptable if you install the Moroso No. 2285 100-psi oil pump relief spring, get .002- to .003-inch end clearance on the rotors and deburr the exterior between the mounting flange and the pump body to prevent cracking.

Even though the main web was deburred and radiused, this 351C block developed the anticipated crack across the bearing saddle and up into the cylinder wall after extended high-performance use.

Two- and four-bolt main caps have the same cross-sectional strength. Strength benefits from the additional two bolts are questionable except for circle-track racing.

The stock oil pump delivers an adequate supply of oil. Just add a high-pressure relief spring and deburr the exterior, as shown, to prevent cracks.

Before I leave the oiling system, I'll specify the use of 20W-50 oil unless you live in a cold climate, and then I'd use 10W-30. Just use care not to rev the engine until it is warmed up and you won't have any trouble.

All 351C cranks are a high nodular iron material. The Boss 351C crank (part No. D1ZZ-6303-A) was balanced slightly different from all the other cranks (part No. D0AZ-6303-A) but you can use either version as long as it is identified with a "2M" code on the counterweight. Just resize the main journals to 2.7480 inches and the rod journals to 2.3088 inches. If you do anything else, Tufftride it. Tufftriding will warp the crank so it will have to be competently straightened afterward. Use the Mr. Gasket No. 1966 neoprene rear main seal or the Ford C90Z-6701-A seal. Use the full-groove TRW main bearings, MS-3010P, with .002- to .0025-inch clearance. Torque the main cap bolts to 100 ft.-lbs. And use the D1AZ-6316-A damper up front. If you're bucks up, the BOSS 351C damper (part No. D2ZZ-6316-A) is better yet, but not absolutely necessary.

The BOSS 351C connecting rod (part No. D1ZZ-6200-A), which is marked D1ZX-AA on the beam, is an excellent rod with a high nickel content and the premium 180,000-psi bolts, but it's more than we really need for the street. Therefore, use the standard rod (part No. D0AZ-6200-A), which is marked D0AE-A on the beam, and simply add the good bolts (part No. D1ZZ-6214-A) and nuts (part No. D1ZZ-6212-A). These premium bolts are the same size, so they're a direct replacement, but install them *before* doing any other rod work.

Rebuild the rods to make sure the hole in the big end is round. Normally I take about .002-inch off the caps and rebore them to .0004- or .0005-inch under the manufacturer's specification (2.4360 inches). Then Magnaflux the rods to check for cracks.

For bearings, use the TRW (Clevite 77) rod bearings CB927P. If you install dowel pins in the rod caps to retain the bearing, use the CB962P inserts. TRW also has bearings, CB961P, that feature the dowel pin hole and .001-inch extra oil clearance. Rod bearing clearance should be .002- to .0025-inch for engines that won't be revved over 6000 rpm, and .0025- to .003-inch for over-6000-rpm operation.

Use the .003-inch oversize Ford pistons (part No. D2ZZ-6108-C). These pistons have a very good skirt design that will run with tight wall clearance. In fact, it has a better skirt than the TRW aftermarket replacement, and TRW makes the Ford pistons! I specified .003-inch oversize because I think the 351C block should always be honed to .003-inch oversize with torque plates to clean everything up. The cylinder walls are quite thin, .130- to .190-inch, so overbores more than .003-inch aren't a good idea. Hone for a piston-to-wall clearance of .003-inch for low-rpm applications and .0035-inch for over-6000-rpm use. Cut the block for a deck height of .019-inch down in the bore.

In the piston, hone the pin hole for .0008-inch clearance. Other than that, the pistons are ready to run as is, but mike all the skirts just to be sure that one hasn't been dropped or damaged during manufacture. When pressing in the pins, use the Sunnen B-200 anti-seize lubricant spray to prevent any galling. You can get it at most engine rebuilding shops or industrial tool supply dealers. You must have a good fixture to hold the piston and rod in perfect alignment during the pin pressing operation, but the engine rebuilder who has the Sunnen

Any of the 351C rods can be used for high performance, although all should be fitted with the BOSS 351C bolts and nuts. Shown here is a stock rod compared to a fully polished version for oval-track racing.

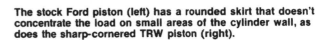

The stock Ford piston (left) has a rounded skirt that doesn't concentrate the load on small areas of the cylinder wall, as does the sharp-cornered TRW piston (right).

The BOSS 351C rod bolt (left) can be distinguished from the stock bolt (right) by the absence of serrations on the shank.

This Sunnen lubricant should be used whenever the pins are pressed into the connecting rods, to prevent galling of either the rod, pin or piston.

spray will probably have the man and the equipment necessary to do this job for you.

Use the Sealed Power/Speed Pro R-9343 ring set. It features a moly-filled 5/64-inch top ring, a cast-iron 5/64-inch second ring and a 3/16-inch oil ring. Ask for the 4.000 + .005-inch oversize set and file the end gaps for a *minimum* of .015-inch on the top rings and .012-inch on the second rings.

Next we'll consider camshafts, since that will determine which heads and valvetrain pieces we use. For vehicles with manual transmissions and rearend ratios of over 3.5:1, or automatics with 4.1:1 or more, use the BOSS 351C solid lifter cam (part No. D1ZZ-6250-B). If a manual trans is used with less than 3.5:1 rearend gear ratio, or an automatic with less than 4.1:1, use the hydraulic lifter CJ cam (part No. D1ZZ-6250-A). And incidentally, if the cam bearings are within specifications in the block, leave 'em alone and don't try to change them.

After selecting a cam, choose the correct 4V, big-port, open-chamber heads (part No. D2ZZ-6049-A for solid lifter cams and part No. D1ZZ-6049-C for hydraulics). These heads will provide approximately 9.2:1 compression with the pistons specified earlier and the .038-inch-thick McCord 6850M head gaskets. Drill the head gaskets as shown in the accompanying diagram.

The valve sizes for these heads are 2.19-inch intakes and 1.71 exhausts. There are two valve designs: multi-groove rotating and single-groove nonrotating. For street durability, the rotating setup is probably the better, but there's not really a lot of difference one way or the other, so I'll give the part numbers for both. They are as follows:

	Multi-Groove (Rotating)	Single-Groove (Nonrotating)
Intake valve	D0AZ-6507-A	D0ZZ-6507-A
Exhaust valve	D0AZ-6505-E	D0ZZ-6505-A
Retainer	D0AZ-6514-A	C9ZZ-6514-A
Keeper	D0AZ-6518-A	C9ZZ-6518-A

For either setup, use the D0OZ-6571-A valve seals and the BOSS 351C valve springs (part No. D0ZZ-6513-A) installed at 1.82 inches with the D0OZ-6A536-A spring seats.

The remainder of the valvetrain pieces are as follows:

	Solid Lifter Cam	Hydraulic Lifter Cam
Lifters	D1ZZ-6500-B	D1AZ-6500-B (anti-pump-up)
Pushrods	D2ZZ-6565-A	D0AZ-6565-A
Rocker arm studs	C9ZZ-6A527-A	C9ZZ-6A527-A
Rocker arm stud nuts	C8ZZ-6A529-B	C8ZZ-6A529-B
Rocker arm fulcrums	C9ZZ-6A528-A	C9ZZ-6A528-A
Rocker arms	C9ZZ-6564-A	C9ZZ-6564-A
Guide plates	C9ZZ-6A564-A	------

Both the rocker arms and the fulcrums should be Tuff-trided to reduce wear and to prevent penetration of the pushrod through the rocker arm.

Now we can button up the engine. Use the D1ZZ-6675-C oil pan. If you're handy with a torch, or know somebody who is, you might want to deepen the pan 1 inch by welding in a section just beneath the gasket flange. This is preferable to just deepening the sump.

On top, use the latest Edelbrock Torker intake manifold with the solid lifter cam and the D1ZZ-9424-G manifold with the hydraulic cam. In either case, use the D0AZ-9433-A intake manifold gasket, which doubles as an oil shield. Atop the manifold the 780-cfm carb (part No. D3ZZ-9510-E for sticks and D0OF-9510-R for automatics) is ideal for use with the hydraulic cam. Solid cam engines can use either the 800-cfm or 850-cfm Holley double-pumpers, R-4780 or R-4781, respectively.

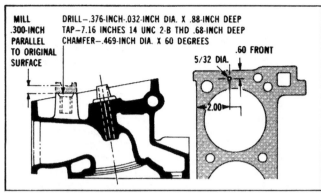

You can achieve improved head gasket durability by drilling a 5/32-inch-diameter hole (as illustrated). This modification is extremely helpful in situations where extended high-rpm situations are encountered. It is not needed for drag racing This illustration shows the slotted pedestal used with 351C heads for use with a hydraulic cam. They can be modified to accept a mechanical cam valve train by milling off .300-inch. Be sure to mill parallel to the bottom of the *slot*, not head.

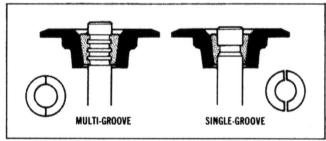

Shown are the two different styles of 351C valves. The multi-groove valve (left) has keepers that bottom against each other so that the valve will be free to rotate. The single-groove design tightly grips the valve stem and no rotation occurs.

This Ford aluminum intake manifold works well with the hydraulic lifter cam and automatic transmissions (see text).

In the ignition department, use the '71 BOSS distributor (part No. D1ZZ-12127-D). If the car has an automatic trans, connect a manifold vacuum line to the vacuum port farthest from the distributor housing on the dual diaphragm vacuum can.

Headers shoud be either 1¾- or 2-inch diameter with 40-inch primary tubes. Standard-transmission cars can gain additional performance by using an aluminum flywheel matched and balanced to the application. Auto-trans cars will benefit by using the '72 351C 4V C-6 torque convertor (part No. D2OZ-7902-A), which has a stall speed of 3000 rpm and excellent top end lockup. This convertor can be identified by a "67", "69" or "CB" code on the front of the unit.

That wraps up our 351C buildup. Of course an engine like this might pose emission certification problems for street use in some states, so check with the authorities before putting your money or the hammer down. ■■

FORDging up a winner

At last, forged cranks are available for the 351C Ford V8

Text & photos by C. J. Baker ■ There's little question that 1973 was the year of the Ford Pintos in Pro Stock drag racing, and '74 looks equally promising. But as with all forms of racing, as engine builders find an ever-growing number of ways to wring power out of a specific engine, component limitations become a hindrance to further progress. This is the case with the stock 351C Ford crankshaft.

Many Ford racers find it desirable to reduce the diameter of the connecting rod journals to either the early-Chevy dimension of two inches or to the late-Chevy 2.1-inch size. When this is done to the stock Ford cast nodular iron crankshaft, two problems arise. First, the crank is critically weakened, and second, the oil passage is so close to the surface of the journal that cracks develop back into the fillet area. When this happens, the crankshaft is doomed to certain failure. Additionally, stroke variation on the stock cast crank is limited to 3.4-3.6 inches.

But now all of these problems have been overcome by Hank Bechtloff, better known to most racers as Hank the Crank. Hank's North Hollywood, California, shop is now producing his own SUP-R-REV 351 forged cranks for the 351C. The new forged crank incorporates many desirable features for race-oriented engines. Because it is a forging rather than a casting, Hank's new crank is inherently stronger, and two-inch-diameter rod journals present no problem. The oil passages are cross-drilled and repositioned to avoid the cracking problem mentioned earlier. Possible stroke combinations vary all the way from 2.85 inches to 3.75 inches. All journals feature radiused fillets and chamfered oil holes, and they are Tufftride heat-treated and polished.

Another problem with the stock cast crank is that it is difficult to balance internally, but Hank's forged crank has two additional center counterweights to solve the dilemma. As with most custom racing crankshafts, the price is high (over $700), but the benefits make it all worthwhile. If you don't believe it, ask the man whose name is inscribed on the crank in the lead photo (Bob Glidden). ■ ■

ABOVE LEFT—Shown from left to right are the stock Ford cast crank, the semi-finished and a completely finished SUP-R-REV 351 forged crank. Note the additional counterweights (arrows) on the forged versions. LEFT—Cutting the stock Ford crank journals to a two-inch diameter not only weakens the crank, but it also invites cracks from the oil passage into the fillet area (dotted lines).

SOUTHERN FRIED FORD

HOW TO BUILD A 570-HP 351C FOR A SUNDAY DRIVE By Mario Rossi **PART 1**

Editor's Note:
There are few forms of auto racing that impose more demands on an engine builder than NASCAR Grand National competition. Not only is it essential for these engines to produce enough power to be competitive; they must also make this power in a specific usable rpm range that is sufficiently wide to accelerate those massive stockers out of the corners and reach peak speeds down the straightaways. But perhaps of even greater importance is the demand on these engines to live under sustained high-output usage—to go 500 miles flat out.

There's quite a difference between building an engine to produce peak power for a matter of seconds, as in drag racing, and one that must perform flawlessly for three and a half hours. Consequently, the talents and knowledge of those men who have accomplished such feats are greatly respected. One such man, Mario Rossi, currently builds engines at the spacious Reed Cams, Inc., facility in Decatur, Georgia. Because Mario's accomplishments include extensive work with the Ford 351 Cleveland engine, we've asked him to outline what is required to turn one of these engines into a NASCAR screamer. His approach is methodical, leaving nothing to chance. It is a procedure that could be applied equally to any make of engine, and therefore, what he has to say is of value to anyone building engines, Ford or not.

I don't build street engines and I don't build drag engines. Consequently, a lot of what I go through to build an engine may seem totally unnecessary to many of you, but believe me, it's attention to little details that usually makes the difference between being in the running at the end of a 500-mile race or pushing the car behind the wall at some point before that. You simply can't take chances or compromise where durability is at stake. What I'll be describing here is a 355-cubic-inch, single four-barrel, NASCAR Grand National engine based on the Ford 351 Cleveland. It will have a bore of 4.020 inches, a 3.50-inch stroke, a billet crank, a mushroom flat-tappet cam and 12.5:1 compression. An engine built *exactly* as follows, using these exact components and procedures, without shortcuts, will produce a reliable 560-to-570 hp at 7000-to-7200 rpm with 445-to-450 ft.-lbs. of torque at 5600-to-5800 rpm. This is equivalent to what the engines in the top-running cars are developing.

The basic foundation of this, or any, engine is the block. Until recently the only suitable block was the 351C-4V block, which has four-bolt main caps. Unfortunately, cylinder wall thickness, block rigidity and main webs thickness were all marginal on these blocks. Additionally, casting quality, in terms of core shift and flashing, along with machining tolerances, left a lot to be desired. Now there's a better block available. It is generally referred to as the Australian block, but that's kind of a misnomer. My understanding is that the

block is cast in the U.S., shipped to Australia for machining, and then shipped back to the U.S. This block has beefier main webs and caps. The caps are high-nodular iron, the cylinder walls are thicker (.165-inch minimum) and more uniform, and the pan rails are thicker for greater rigid-

The top block is a production 351C-4V version, whereas the bottom one is the Australian block. Compare the main webs and the pan rail in terms of material thickness.

ity. Core shift seems to be virtually nil, and the castings are very clean, with little flashing. They also seemed to be machined to very close tolerances. These blocks bear a casting number, XE-182540, and they are currently available from either Gapp & Roush Performance in Livonia, Michigan, or Hank the Crank in North Hollywood, California.

These Australian blocks are fairly expensive, and due to the extra material, they are considerably heavier than the conventional 351C blocks, but the advantages so outweigh these drawbacks, both in durability and the mandatory preparation time, that in my opinion, there is absolutely no reason to even consider using the conventional block. However, even as good as it is, I still check the Australian block meticulously before beginning any preparation work.

I begin by removing all the plugs in the block (oil passage and freeze plugs). The cam bearings, which come with the bare block, are also removed. I examine the block closely for any production flaws, core sand in the water jackets, etc. The oil passages are inspected for machining chips or restrictions. They are also checked to verify that all passages are drilled to the correct diameter and depth.

Next, the main bearing saddles are checked for proper alignment. Then the caps are torqued to the correct specification and the main bearing bores are checked for diameter and concentricity. Each lifter bore is checked for diameter and to verify that its centerline is perpendicular to

Before installing the bearing inserts, the edges are chamfered to clear the crank journal radii and the oil slot is enlarged to correspond to the oil passage indicated. Don't overdo it. Note that restrictors have also been placed in the passages supplying the cam bearings to limit oil flow in that area.

When modifying the block to accept a dry-sump oiling system with remote oil filters, it is necessary to plug or cap this oil drainback hole to prevent oil from leaking out of the engine. Rossi generally uses a small aluminum plate, as shown, to accomplish this. Although not shown, the hole in the front of the block for the dipstick tube is also plugged when a dry sump is used.

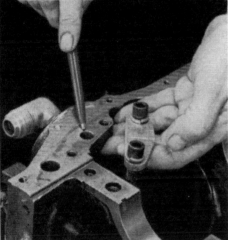

All honing is done in a Sunnen CK-10 using 1½-inch head plates torqued to 110 ft.-lbs. Sunnen JHU-820 stones (400 grit) are used with a honing load of approximately 30 on the machine's meter to produce the final wall finish of 8 to 13 microinches without burnishing.

The billet crank, steel rods, pistons and pins are all from Hank the Crank. Note the use of heavy metal to achieve proper balance while keeping the counterweights smooth and streamlined.

The Ford 302 harmonic balancer (part No. C8FE-6316-B) is used, but the stock counterweight (left) is machined away, since it is not needed with the fully counterweighted crankshaft.

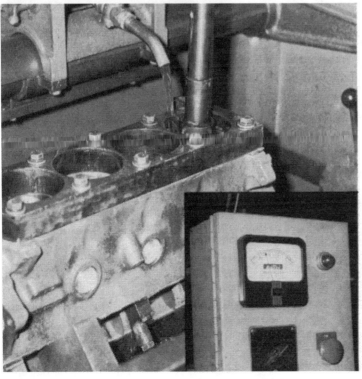

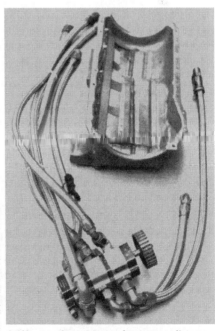

A Weaver three-stage dry-sump oil pump with 1.7-inch gears is used with a special Aviad oil pan. Note the extensive use of screens and scrapers in shallow oil pan.

the centerline of the camshaft. The cylinder bores are similarly checked to verify that they are perpendicular to the crankshaft centerline. This is crucial. If the bore is canted slightly to the front or rear, the piston pin will inevitably hammer out the pin locks and destroy the engine. If they cant up or down, the piston will tend to cock in the bore, cracking the cylinder wall, causing bearing wear, etc. In the event that you do find a slight misalignment and the cylinder bores are to be overbored, such as I do by .020-inch, then it *may* be possible to machine out that misalignment, using a boring machine that locates off the crankshaft centerline. Other items checked for perpendicularity are the cam thrust surface and the bellhousing mating face. They must be perpendicular to the camshaft centerline and the crankshaft centerline, respectively.

All of this checking is very time-consuming, but it is essential in terms of durability. Additionally, you are determining if you have a good block to work with. If you find a problem, then you have the option of fixing it or getting another block before proceeding. In checking many of the Australian blocks, I find that most have turned out to be "dead on" perfect, but occasionally you will find a small problem, so check it carefully. Now we're ready to begin the deburring and machining operations, along with the correction of any problems.

First I grind off all casting flash and sharp edges. (I don't like to cut my hands while working on engines.) Any rough edges or stress risers, particularly in the main web area, are carefully radiused or smoothed to reduce the likelihood of cracks. All threads are chased with a tap, including the head bolt threads, which are also checked for depth to verify that the head bolts will not bottom. If the block requires align-honing of the main bearing bores, that is done next. Then the bottoms of the lifter bores are spotfaced to accept the mushroom tappets.

When you are spotfacing the lifter bores, they must be cut sufficiently deep to allow .030- to .040-inch clearance between the bottom of the lifter and the nose of the cam at peak lift to allow for overrev protection. Another quick way to get adequate clearance is to cut them deep enough so that a straightedge laid on the cam bearing saddles (without the bearings in place) will clear the tappets.

Next the block is bored and honed for a finished size that will give a .009- to .0085-inch piston-to-wall clearance. (I'll cover the pistons in detail later on, but now I'll detail the boring/honing procedure.) All boring and honing is done with 1½-inch headplates installed, using the exact type of head gasket that will be run on the engine and torquing the bolts to 110 ft.-lbs. The main caps are also installed and torqued. I prefer to use studs in place of the stock capscrews, but the capscrews are acceptable. The block is bored to within .010-inch of the finished size. It is then set up in a Sunnen CK-10 and honed to within .0015- to .002-inch of the finish size, using the Sunnen JHU-625 or JHU-5525 stones. It is then finished to size with the Sunnen JHU-820 stones, maintaining a stone load of 25 to 30 on the machine's honing load meter. This produces a very smooth finish of 8-to-13 microinches without burnishing.

The next major block machining operation is the squaring and decking of the block, but to do this you'll have to have the crank, rods, pistons, pins and bearings, so I'll cover those before getting into decking.

Actually, the crank, rods and pistons are some of the simplest parts of the engine from the standpoint of preparation, since they are all supplied by Hank the Crank. I use the billet, fully counterweighted, Tufftrided crank. Hank also has a fully reworked cast crank available for less money, but even with all of the tricks, these cast cranks are good for no more than one superspeedway race. On the other hand, the billet cranks will last five or six races (some have even been run 8 to 10 races), so in the long run the billet is cheaper and more reliable. The billet crank has large radii, which means that the bearings must be chamfered. The TRW/Clevite 77 fully grooved inserts are what I prefer to use, since quality control and sizing seem to be very good. The oil slot in the upper shell is also opened slightly, as shown, to improve oil flow. About the only thing to check once you receive the HTC crank is straightness, since it may have gotten bent in shipment. If it is within .001-inch, it is okay.

Hank also supplies the steel rods, which are of his own design. If the engine is being built for either Daytona or Talladega, where a narrower rpm range can be utilized, 6.0-inch rods are used. For all other tracks, the rod length is 5.80 inches. These rods are bushed on the small end. They come completely finished, including SPS bolts, but check 'em for length, as well as straightness and concentricity.

The pistons are a BRC/HTC design. They feature a high-silicone-content aluminum alloy, a 10cc dome and a wide skirt, and the top ring groove is .425-inch down from the deck to allow adequate material above the groove and the intake valve pocket to prevent failure (.100-inch after cutting for valve relief). The pistons are available for either the 6.0- or 5.8-inch rods, and they already have all of the necessary pin oiling holes. HTC lightweight taper pins are used and are retained with double .043-inch Spiroloks.

With the crank, rods and pistons on hand, a trial fit can be made to determine block deck height. This is done by installing the crank and fitting the main bearings. Using bore gauges and micrometers, get a true main bearing clearance of .0025-to .00275-inch, and then mark the inserts so that you can put them back with the right cap and journal on final assembly. Fit the pistons to the rods with a pin clearance of .0008-inch in both the rod and piston. The end clearance on the pins should be zero. After running, this pin end-play will open up to .003- to .005-inch, which is correct. Next, fit the pistons in the bores, using plenty of oil, but no rings. Set the rod bearing clearance at .0025-inch, again using TRW/Clevite 77 bearing inserts. At this point, the piston deck height can be checked to determine how much the block will have to be machined.

Check rod side clearance at this time too. It should be .017- to .020-inch. If it isn't, get it. Then disassemble everything and set it aside.

The deck height that we will want is .010-inch down in the bores. It is also important that the deck be cut exactly perpendicular to the cylinder centerlines. This is usually accomplished by taking a light cut on the block to square it, and then a second cut is taken to achieve the correct deck height. Most decking equipment leaves a suitable surface finish for good gasket sealing.

The final steps in the block preparation include a light chamfer at both the top and bottom of the cylinder bore. It will also be necessary to install oil restrictor plugs (see sidebar).

This completes the machine work on the block, but we're still a long way from final assembly. The piston domes still have to be smoothed, valve reliefs must be checked, and if necessary deepened, and the rotating assembly has to be balanced. We'll cover all of that, along with the heads, valvetrain, induction system, etc., next month. In the meantime, there are a few items that are still required for the lower end. I use the HTC external oiling system, since it bypasses all of the shortcomings of the stock Ford oiling system (see sidebar). However, the oil pump used is a Weaver dry-sump unit with two scavenge and one pressure stage. Each stage uses 1.7-inch gears. A few tips on this system include a 1-inch-i.d. line from the oil reservoir to the pressure stage and dual ¾-inch-i.d. lines from the scavenge pumps to the tank. Use only straight or 45-degree fittings in all of the oil lines. If a 90-degree fitting must be used, select a free-flowing aircraft fitting. The pump is driven with Gilmer belt, using a 26-tooth gear on the crank and a 32-tooth gear on the pump.

Ground clearance problems prevent the use of an ideal pan, in terms of depth, but the pan used does have a full-length screened windage tray and scrapers. Pickups are provided for three scavenging stages, although only two are used. This Aviad pan is available from Reed Cams, Inc.

When you've completed all of the required machining, do a super-thorough cleaning job on the block. This will include using bottle and rifle brushes in the oil and water passages, along with liberal use of solvent and detergents. If a steam cleaner is available, use it, particularly on the cylinder bores. When a block is properly cleaned, you should be able to dry it off and wipe a clean white handkerchief in the cylinder bores without *any* trace of gray appearing on the cloth.

I'm sure this is enough to keep you busy until next month, so start gathering the pieces. It all takes a lot of time. **HR**

LUBING THE CLEVELAND

The design of the lubrication system in the 351 Cleveland engine seems to have its priorities reversed, supplying oil first to the lifters and cam bearings, and then delivering whatever oil volume and pressure is left to the main bearings, crank and rod bearings. This provides a lot of opportunity for both pressure and volume to bleed off before reaching the critical bearings. To offset the problem, many engine builders resort to running excessively high oil pressure in the Cleveland (over 100 psi) to ensure adequate oil to the crank. But there are better ways to do it.

One of the better cures for the Cleveland seems to be the installation of an external oiling system, like the one offered by Hank the Crank. This system, in conjunction with a series of metering and restrictor plugs, delivers full oil volume and pressure to the rear of the block, where it is manifolded directly to the main bearings through a set of pressed-in sleeves in the lifter galley. The system works with either a wet- or dry-sump oil system.

An alternative is to restrict the oil going to the lifters with the conventional oiling system by sleeving the lifter bores. Hank also offers a kit to do this. Either way, it is much-needed help for this engine. ■

Restrictor plugs are inserted to limit oil to the cam bearings and left lifter bank.

Although it is an earlier design, plumbing in this kit indicates how oil is routed.

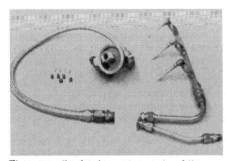
These are the basic components of the external oiling kit in its latest form.

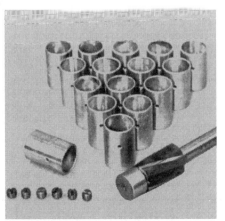
If the external oiling kit isn't used, the lifter bores can be sleeved to limit oil.

SOUTHERN FRIED FORD

CONCLUDING THE IN-DEPTH DISCUSSION OF HOW TO
BUILD A GRAND NATIONAL-TYPE 351C FORD   **PART 2**
By Mario Rossi

Last month we managed to cover the majority of our 355-inch 351C Ford short-block, but looking back, I feel that I should mention a few points. First off, when fitting the crankshaft in the block to check clearances, make sure you have .004- to .006-inch of crankshaft end play. Next, the flywheel that I recommend with this combination is a 22-pound lightweight steel version (part No. GR7W-6380-A) from Gapp and Roush. And last, I recommend Magnafluxing or some other inspection process. Magnafluxing, X-ray and Zy-Glo checking is good insurance, and absolutely essential on a rebuild or overhaul.

In this business of racing, there's nothing quite as constant as change. We're always looking at new things and exploring new ways of achieving greater power levels and durability. Since Part 1, we've done considerable dyno work and found something of interest. If you recall, I specified using 6-inch rods only for high-speed tracks like Daytona and Talladega. However, in light of increased torque and horsepower figures we've been able to achieve through a broader rpm range, I now recommend a 6-inch rod for all applications except very short ½-mile tracks, where the 5.8-inch rod should be used. Not only does this combination produce more power, but the longer-length rod improves piston and cylinder wall durability. The difference isn't big, but if you've got the choice, go the longer route.

When we left off last month, we'd done everything we could without the cam and heads, but to proceed, those pieces will have to be obtained next. The cylinder heads are another thing that take little preparation on the part of the engine builder. They are supplied, completely ready to as-semble, by Reed Cams, Decatur, Georgia. These heads are based on 6F18 castings and are fully ported. They flow 330 to 340 cfm on the intakes, 215 to 220 cfm on the exhausts, measured at .600-inch valve lift at a depression of 28 inches of water on a Superflow bench. The ports are not welded, although the heat riser opening is welded closed. These heads are supplied with 2.19-inch-diameter Ford/TRW titanium intake valves with 11/32-inch stems and Manley 1.71-inch (11/32-inch stems) stainless steel exhausts. The valves are cut with a three-angle valve job, and cast-iron guides are installed with .002-inch clearance on the intakes and .0025-inch on the exhausts. Perfect Circle rubber valve seals with Teflon inserts control valve guide oiling.

The combustion chambers on these heads are held between 64 and 65cc, which when used in conjunction with the .010-inch down deck

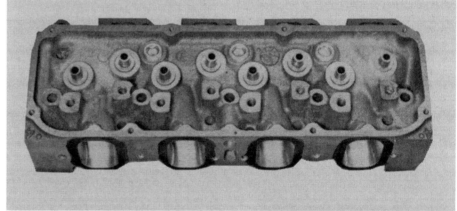

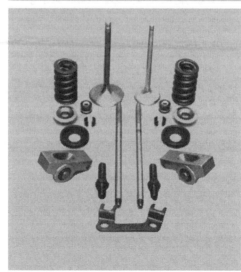

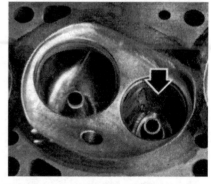

Reed Cams modified the heads, welding the heat riser closed and fully porting and polishing them for maximum flow. The heads are assembled with titanium intake and stainless steel exhaust valves, Reed springs and components, and roller rockers.

height, a piston dome of 8 to 10cc and a .035-inch-thick head gasket, will yield a compression ratio of 12.2:1 to 12.5:1. For additional strength, the Ford heads also must have the combustion chambers "pinned" (see sidebar) to prevent cracking during endurance racing. Reed Cams does this as part of their normal head preparation. To complete the heads, Reed steel spring cups, titanium retainers, hardened steel locks and valve springs are used. The valve springs, which are Reed No. 2260 outers and No. 2261 inners with a flat damper, have 145 pounds seat pressure and 360 to 380 pounds open pressure, depending on the maximum valve lift. They are installed at a height of 1.87 inches.

The head gaskets used on this engine, McCord No. 6850M versions, have a compressed thickness of .035-inch. This gasket is stamped to indicate which end must go toward the front of the engine. It is possible to install them backward, so be careful or the water jacket openings will be misaligned. I also drill a 3/16-inch hole in the gasket corresponding to the water jacket (as shown) at the front of the engine, to promote more

even cooling. On final assembly, I also coat the block, head and both sides of the gasket with high-temperature aluminum paint to ensure a good seal.

The next area of concern is the

cam and valvetrain. Once again, these pieces come from Reed Cams. We are presently using cams with intake and exhaust durations of 274° and 280° (at .050-inch lift) for Daytona and Talladega and 268° and 276°

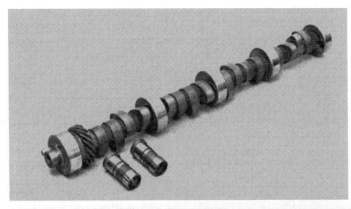

The Reed mushroom tappet cam provides flow and minimal duration for peak power across a wide rpm range.

THE RIGHT TRACK

Another important aspect of cylinder head preparation has to do with the type of track the heads will be used on. For example, when the heads are ported and flowed, flow is checked at valve lifts of .300-, .400-, .500- and .600-inch and a flow curve is plotted. If the heads are prepared to produce optimum flow at .600-inch lift, then the flow at the lower lifts tends to be somewhat less than if the heads are ported to achieve the highest possible average flow at all valve lifts. The difference is that a port that flows exceedingly well at .600-inch lift usually has to have a bigger cross-sectional area. Consequently, the velocity of flow is slower at the lower lifts, thus making the low lift flow sort of lazy. Therefore, heads for superspeedways, such as Daytona or Talladega, where a very narrow rpm range is utilized, are ported solely for peak flow at the maximum valve lift checking specification of .600-inch. Heads for the shorter tracks, where a wider rpm range is needed, along with quick throttle response and torque coming off the corners, are ported for the best average flow, even though peak flow at .600-inch may be off 10 or 20 cfm. ●

KEEPING A HEAD

Preparing the Ford 351C cylinder heads for endurance racing requires a bit of extra effort. To withstand 3½ hours of continuous racing, the combustion chambers and surrounding gasket surface need to be beefed-up to prevent cracks and blown gaskets. Such reinforcement is called pinning, and it consists of eight support studs screwed into the head until they bear against the backside of the chamber and gasket surface. The accompanying photos indicate where they are placed. One stud is inserted at the end of the head, passing

through the water jacket adjacent to the intake valve. Three other studs are installed by drilling and tapping through three of the four exhaust rocker arm stud bosses. The fourth stud boss is not used, because of the heat riser passage directly beneath it. The four remaining studs are installed right through the gasket surface of the head, passing through the water jacket and bottoming against the exhaust port floors. The head is then surfaced to cut these four studs perfectly level with the rest of the gasket surface. ●

Eight pins are installed in each head. One pin is screwed through the end of the head (left), while four others are inserted directly through the gasket surface (circles) to bear against the bottom of the exhaust ports to provide additional support to the gasket surface, which is milled flat after the pinning is completed. The remaining three pins are inserted through three of the intake rocker stud bosses until they bear against the gasket surface at the points indicated (Xs). Note that no pin is installed at the middle of the head because of the blocked heat riser in that location.

SOUTHERN FRIED FORD

for the short- and intermediate-length tracks. These cams are ground on 106° lobe centers, with lifts of .675-inch for the intake and .685-inch on the exhaust (long duration) and .657-inch and .676-inch for the short-track grind. Both are mushroom tappet cams. Of course cam design and technology are constantly evolving, so by the time you read this, even better profiles may be available, so check with Reed for the best cam for your particular application. Since gear drives aren't NASCAR-legal, I use a Cloyes True-Roller chain and sprocket, but if you can legally use a gear drive, do so.

Because of the mushroom tappet cams, limiting cam "walk" (end play) is critical to prevent the tappets from overlapping onto adjacent cam lobes. This is done by machining either the cam sprocket or the thrust plate. I try to hold the end play to .002-inch, but up to .010-inch is acceptable.

The remainder of the valvetrain consists of the Reed mushroom tappets (supplied with the cam), with a 1-inch face and an .872-inch body. The Reed ⅜-inch-diameter 4130 steel alloy pushrods, Reed 7/16-inch, heat-treated 4330 steel alloy rocker studs, Harland Sharp 1.73:1 aluminum roller rocker arms and a Reed rocker stud girdle (features adjusting nuts with positive locking setscrews) complete the assembly, along with stock Ford pushrod guide plates.

With all of these pieces on hand, it is time for another trial assembly to check proper valvetrain geometry

and piston-to-valve clearance. Install the cam bearings, the mushroom tappets for one cylinder, the cam and cam drive (degreeing the cam at the straight-up, on-time position), the crank and one piston/rod assembly without rings. Bolt on the head for the cylinder being checked and install the remaining valvetrain pieces for that cylinder, setting the valve lash to normal running clearances. Using checking springs, measure the piston-to-valve clearance at the closest point, which usually occurs 8 to 12° BTDC for the exhaust and 8 to 12° ATDC for the intake valve (on the overlap stroke). With today's state-of-the-art mushroom cam designs, with their inherently quick "off-the-seat" action, it is almost always necessary to remachine the valve pockets in the pistons to get a

minimum of .080-inch and .100-inch clearance on the intake and exhaust valves, respectively. If you don't take the time to check this and to get the proper clearance, don't complain when you stuff the valves into the piston domes and junk the engine. If you plan on swapping back and forth between cam designs, set the piston-to-valve clearance with the wildest grind, which will ensure adequate clearance for milder cams.

After cutting the additional valve relief depths, the tops of the pistons should be deburred and radiused to remove any sharp edges and to promote low-lift flow and flame propagation within the combustion chambers. This is also a good time to get the rings and check them for land clearance and end gap. I use the Sealed Power/Speed Pro rings, since they

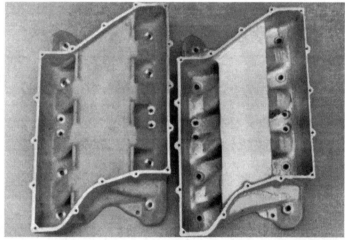

The Bud Moore box manifold is modified (right) to smooth and turn the flow into the runners, which are balanced and matched as much as possible. Notice how the bottom runner wall, in particular, has been moved out.

Before and after comparison of the piston after decking, valve pocket cutting, smoothing and polishing.

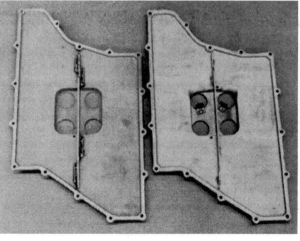

The manifold lid is also modified with an extended divider, flow tabs and directional radii adjacent to two of the four openings. Extensive flow bench is required to achieve peak flow and equal distribution on these manifolds.

have shown consistently good results in this type of application. The top ring is the BR-18PF-12 +.025, 1/16-inch ductile iron, plasma-sprayed, moly-filled, conventional-twist, barrel-faced version—end-gapped at .014-inch. End gaps are measured ½-inch down the bore, with head plates torqued to spec. The oil ring is the SS-50U-567 +.025 low-tension 3/16-inch version. Side clearance on both the top and second moly rings should be .001-inch; the ring groove depth should be such that the face of the ring can be pressed back between zero and .004-inch below the ring land. Under no circumstances should the ring extend beyond the ring land when fully bottomed.

With all the basic engine components gathered, fitted and machined, have the rotating and reciprocating assemblies balanced to 50 percent. I don't subscribe to overbalancing for engines of this type. The final step is to make sure everything is meticulously clean and begin final assembly. Remember that when using a mushroom tappet cam, the first thing that must be installed in the block are the mushroom tappets. Use standard Ford crankshaft end seals and be sure to install the main and rod bearings on the same journals they were fitted to earlier. The SPS capscrews in the connecting rods should be torqued 90 to 95 ft.-lbs., and a good lubricant should be used on the threads and under the capscrew head. I use a mixture of light oil and molybdenum disulfide. If you've got the equipment to measure it, rod bolt (capscrew) stretch is a better indicator of proper tightening than torque. The proper stretch is .004- to .0045-inch. I also use the moly/oil mixture on all bearings and rubbing surfaces during assembly.

Initially install the cam at ½-degree advanced and then recheck it after the heads are in place with all of the valvetrain installed and the valves lashed to the normal specification. The strain placed on the timing chain by the valve springs normally retards the cam about ½-degree, thus putting the cam straight up, where it belongs. If that's not where it is under these conditions, get it there.

Another tip on assembly is to pin the freeze plugs so that they can't pop out. The Waterman Racing Engines aluminum freeze plugs, which incorporate an O-ring, along with a small retaining bar that positively bolts the plug into place, are an alternative.

All that's left now is the final dress-

up equipment. The first item to consider is the intake manifold. To date, the Bud Moore box manifold has shown the best power and torque for the 351C in this type of racing. The box design yields itself to the wider bore spacing of the 4500 Dominator series of carburetors.

Reed does a lot of work to the Bud Moore manifold to improve flow and distribution. Ridges are removed, radii ground and runners reshaped. To do it properly, the distributor even has to be reworked to clear the modified manifold. Other tests have shown that more power can probably be obtained using a properly re-worked 4150-series carb, if a good manifold can be developed to work with the standard-flange Holley carb. The actual carburetor I use is supplied by Reed Cams. This 4500 has the mandatory 1 11/16-inch restrictor rings, but it is completely flowed and matched on Reed's flow bench. The standard Ford intake gasket set that uses the one-piece oil shield/gasket is used in bolting it all together.

The heads are topped off with either stamped steel or cast aluminum valve covers. I prefer the Ridgeway ribbed cast aluminum covers, since they are sufficiently rigid to support the necessary breather tubes, quick-disconnect oil fitting and dry-sump vent that must be used.

The water pump is modified by cutting down the o.d. of the impellers electric fuel pump, position one at

The distributor shaft and housing must be extended to clear the modified manifold.

about ½-inch. This is assuming the use of the Boss 302 cast-iron impeller. This reduces cavitation and slows the water circulation for better cooling at high engine speeds. It also releases an extra 5 horsepower at racing speeds. But the fuel pump is something else altogether. The stock Ford mechanical fuel pump has a durability problem, but we're restricted to mechanical pumps. Consequently, Bud Moore has contracted with Carter to distribute specially made Carter mechanical pumps. This pump is a must, but be sure to take your checkbook when buying one. If you can legally run an

the rear of the car too.

The rules also require that a production type of ignition be used. If you can find one, use the Ford magnetic impulse transistorized unit, which has a tach drive distributor. These units are rare and expensive, but they work well. The plug wire is silicone-jacketed 8mm by Jack Cotton. Champion BL-57 plugs are selected for the superspeedways, and BL-60 for short tracks. In both cases, they are gapped at .025-inch. As with the fuel pump situation, if you can legally run an aftermarket electronic ignition, do it.

The final item to consider is headers. I use 2-inch-diameter primaries, 34 inches long, feeding into a 3½-inch collector. The tailpipe is also 3½ inches in diameter, usually between 40 and 50 inches long. However, 16 to 18 inches behind the primaries I install a 3-inch-diameter "H" pipe between the collectors. This fools the exhaust system, creating a situation similar to the collectors opening to atmosphere at that point instead of into the tailpipes. This is good for 8 to 10 ft.-lbs. of torque in the midrange.

That about wraps up our southern-fried 351C Ford. It's an expensive engine to build, but any Grand National engine is. Properly done, it's a durable and powerful engine, capable of winning races in the right chassis with the right driver. And you just can't ask for more than that. ●

A 3/16-inch gasket hole here improves cooling. The dipstick hole is plugged too.

The Australian block doesn't have this hole for the clutch linkage. Be sure to drill and tap it before installing the engine.

MORE MUSCLE FOR FORD'S 351

THE SECRET TO BUILDING A GOOD STREET ENGINE IS COMPONENT COMPATIBILITY

HOT ROD BUDGET ENGINE BUILDUP

By Gray Baskerville

There isn't a hot rodder alive who hasn't been interested in bolting some real horseflash onto his otherwise dead player. "The trouble is," says Joe Sherman, low-buck engine builder extraordinary, "too many guys waste a lot of money buying parts they don't need. And there are plenty of shrewd counter-men who will take advantage of their ignorance."

Edelbrock's Jim McFarland sec-onds the emotion. "Detroit designs their various powerplants around a certain mix of factory parts. These parts control induction, camshaft tim-ing and exhaust gases. Unfortunate-

FORD'S FINE FAMILY OF 351S

Introduced in 1975 to simplify assem-bly-line procedures and parts inter-changeability, Ford's 351M, or "Modi-fied," motors are actually "high-block" or "raised-deck" family companions to the long-stroke corporate 400. Posi-tive identification prior to starting work with any of these powerplants is abso-lutely necessary, because although many of an M's pieces will fit a 400, only a few interchange with Ford's identical-displacement Cleveland and Windsor motors. Both the 351M and the 400-incher can be visually identified by a ½-inch-wide by 1-inch-high verti-cal rib cast into the engine block at the immediate left (from the driver's seat) of the distributor. Experienced Ford floggers may also be able to spot the extra inch of material at the taller blocks' deck surfaces, from which the engine derives its high-block designa-tion. Engines known to be factory-fitted to various FoMoCo car and truck models can be positively identified as to displacement by matching the fifth digit in the vehicle's identification or serial number with the corresponding number in that particular year and model's service manual. **HR**

ly, the performance enthusiast who seeks to improve the output of his or her vehicle tends to be more interested in looking for big numbers than adding to the efficiency of these components."

The problem is simple. Few hot rodders are honest with themselves. Instead of taking the time to figure out what rpm range their engine usually operates in, or what kind of fuel economy they would like to achieve, or if it's torque rather than horsepower they want, they operate under the assumption that if they bolt on a set of headers, add an aftermarket intake manifold, attach a 4-barrel carburetor, recurve the distributor, and eventually stick in a high-performance camshaft, they'll end up with a significant power gain. That isn't necessarily true.

The fact of the matter is that most of us don't have the facilities to test these "efficiency mixes." We rely on word-of-mouth claims, or read about unbelievable performance figures. Most of these claims are pure bench racing; you know, wishful thinking. What we really need is some hard information, a form of "when the green flag drops, the bull stops." Consequently, HOT ROD has decided to take the bull by the horns—the first "bull" will be in the form of a late-model, 351-inch, closed-chamber Cleveland Ford (designated the "M" series), followed by similar articles dealing with a 350-inch Chevrolet V8 and a 360-inch MoPar in subsequent issues—and do one of our old "Prove it on the Dyno" bits. (Note: Some of the following modifications may not be legal for street-driven ve-

hicles in your state.)

Now before we could do it on the dyno, we had to find a mule. That particular piece of horsepower was discovered loafing in HOT ROD Publisher Holly Hedrich's '77 Ford Ranchero. However, the two-year-old V8 was more than tired and had to be completely rebuilt and blueprinted before it could be lowered onto Edelbrock's hook. According to Kurt Hooker, Edelbrock's dyno technician and the guy who rebuilt Holly's hound, "It wasn't in too good a shape. We hot-tanked the block, straightened the bores with a Speed-Pro-recommended No. 825-grit Sunnen hone (used in conjunction with SP's moly ring combination), and took .005-inch off the deck. While the main bearings were no problem, the rod bearings were

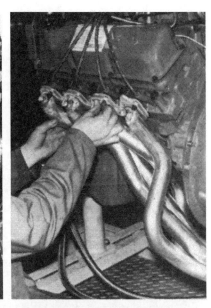

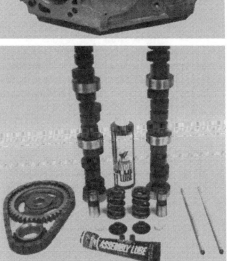

Stock 351M block was decked (.005-inch), had bores straightened and honed; the lifter bores were cleaned up; and it was painted with Rustoleum damp-proof primer. Crane supplied high-rpm Fireball 302A and HT-288-2-NC mid-range cams.

After break-in procedure that involved varying throttle settings for three hours, Kurt Hooker installed a set of Champion RBL 17Ys. Accel igniter was given a total of 24 degrees advance at 3800 rpm. Hooker headers made a big improvement in torque, picking up 14 lbs.-ft. at 2750 over stocker. A 600-cfm Holley carburetor was used in conjunction with both Edelbrock manifolds.

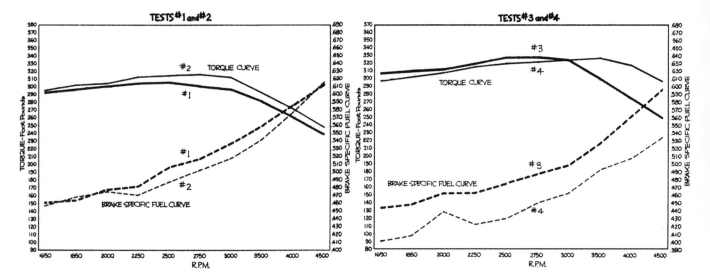

TESTS #1 and #2

TESTS #3 and #4

TORQUE CURVE

BRAKE SPECIFIC FUEL CURVE

shot, because there was too much crush. We also cleaned up the pistons and Magnafluxed all the moving parts, then shot-peened and polished the rod beams, and miked the crank for straightness and roundness.

"Once we dropped in the crank and checked the bearing clearance (.002-inch), I covered the end seals with RTV Silicone to keep them from possibly leaking oil, then torqued down the main caps to 105 ft.-lbs. I also checked the end play (.004-inch) and connecting rod clearance (.015-inch) prior to torquing the rod caps to 45 ft.-lbs. By the way, the ⅜-inch nuts were all cracked and failed the 'Mag,' so we replaced them with new ones. As for the cylinder heads, we simply cleaned up the ports, gave them a good valve job, checked the guides, made sure we had 90 pounds of seat pressure, and torqued them down (in an inside-out sequence) to 105 ft.-lbs. The lubrication is stock; we torqued the stock intake to 25 ft.-lbs."

What "Hook" didn't tell you was

that he augered the crank dampener onto the snout with an 8-pound hammer.

In essence, the plan was to design an induction, cam and exhaust system to produce a significant increase in the engine's torque range that one would encounter under normal driving conditions. To determine what would be best, we thought we would home in on both the engine's torque curve and its Brake Specific Fuel Curve, to measure its combustion efficiency. Torque was considered important, because that's what you feel on the seat of your pants. The Brake Specific Fuel Curve (BSFC) is determined by dividing uncorrected horsepower into how many pounds of fuel are being consumed, then finding out the ratio of burned fuel to power output. For example, a .453 figure means .453-pound of fuel burned per horsepower at a given rpm. In a nutshell, all the BSFC tells you is how much fuel the engine is using to produce maximum torque. If an engine uses 100 pounds of fuel per hour to

produce 1000 ft.-lbs. of torque, then it's more efficient than an engine that uses 150 pounds of fuel to produce the same amount of torque.

Our game plan was almost as simple. We would start by breaking in and baselining the 351 Ford to determine how fuel-efficient the V8 was in its stock configuration, then proceed from there in typical hot-rodding fashion; that is, add a set of exhaust headers, stick in a recurved distributor, switch to an aftermarket intake manifold supporting a 4-barrel carburetor, and finally, make a cam change. In addition to these bolt-ons or bolt-ins, we thought it would be interesting to put together two basic packages. The first would be our high-rpm combination that would feature a set of Hooker headers, one of Accel's distributors, an Edelbrock Streetmaster intake manifold/600-cfm Holley 4160 carburetor (part No. 8006) 4-barrel induction system, and a Crane Fireball 302A hydraulic cam. The second combination would be more conservative and would employ the same headers, with an additional 3-inch extension of the collectors to improve low-end torque, the same distributor, an Edelbrock SP2P intake manifold/8006 Holley combo, and a low- to mid-range Crane HT-288-2-NC hydraulic cam.

TEST NO. 1: After a three-hour break-in period, the baseline run was made, using the stock 2-barrel carburetor. As you can see by the accompanying graph, the 351's maximum torque (306 lbs.-ft. @ 2500 rpm) featured a BSFC of .506. For you horsepower freaks, this run netted 207 horsepower at 4500 rpm.

TEST NO. 2: The only addition to the otherwise stock Ford M was bolting on a set of Hooker No. 6125 headers. These pipes feature

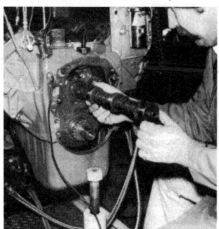

Henry Walther of Crane Cams installs the Fireball 302A. Cam timing killed bottom-end torque, but allowed the 351M to churn out 302 horses at 5000 rpm.

"Hook" gets ready to slap on the Edelbrock SP2P intake manifold. Combination with stock cam put out 333 lbs.-ft. of torque @ 2750—a jump of 27 over OEM 2-barrel system.

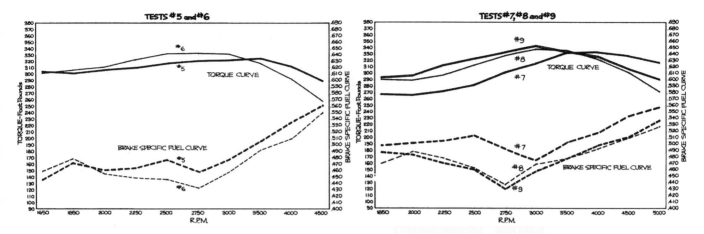

1¾-inch-by-31-inch-long tubes that dump into a 3x10-inch-long collector. Now look at the torque jump all the way through the entire rpm range. Obviously, a reduction in back pressure resulted in a maximum torque figure of 316 lbs.-ft. @ 2750, while the BSFC reads .502, only a .004-pound decrease over the stocker at 2500 rpm. Horsepower was 214 @ rpm.

TEST NO. 3:
The next step was to replace the stock electronic ignition with an Accel No. 34202 distributor recurved to give 24 degrees of advance at 3800 rpm, or a total of 36 degrees (with 12 degrees in the crank) overall. We also twisted in a set of standard-gap Champion RBL 17Y plugs gapped at .032-inch. Stockers were Champion RBL 17Y6 gapped at .060-inch (for the electronic ignition). Again the 351M liked the change. Maximum torque was 327 lbs.-ft. @ 2750, and the BSFC dropped to .487 at the same rpm. Horsepower was 215 @ 4500 rpm.

TEST NO. 4:
Now we added a Streetmaster fitted with a 600-cfm Holley carburetor. The only changes made to the carburetor were to richen the primaries to No. 65 Holley jets and to change the secondary metering plate to a No. 12, .003-inch richer than stock. However, the overall torque curve suffered considerably, and we moved the curve up to 3500 rpm. Then the corrected horsepower figure climbed from 215, with the stock induction system, to 256 @ 4500 rpm. BSFC was .493 at maximum torque.

TEST NO. 5:
Because of the increased flow characteristic of the Streetmaster, the carburetor was further altered to provide more gas; the primaries were richened up an additional two jet sizes (No. 67), but the secondary metering plate (No. 12) was retained. Torque dropped off 4 lbs.-ft. @ 3500 rpm, and the BSFC went up to .505 at the same rpm. Maximum horsepower at 4500 was 251. The feeling here was that while the runner moved more air, the engine's volumetric efficiency was lessened. In fact, it would produce a "hole." What was need was more cam timing.

TEST NO. 6:
We now switched to Edelbrock's new SP2P intake manifold (designed to work with stock cam timing and jetting, and featuring a 4000-rpm ceiling), and the carburetor was returned to its box-stock setting (No. 62 jets primary, No. 39 secondary metering plate). Maximum torque jumped up to 333 lbs.-ft. @ 2750, while the BSFC dropped down to .431 at the same rpm. Horsepower was 222 @ 4500 rpm. This was clearly a significant change in engine efficiency.

TEST NO. 7:
This was the test we all had looked forward to. In essence, this was to be our high-horsepower run, and it featured a combination that included Crane's Fireball 302A hydraulic cam. According to Crane, this particular grind exhibits a fair idle, with good low- to mid-range torque and horsepower. The recommended usage of this cam is that it be combined with a small 4 barrel carburetor, an aftermarket intake manifold, recurved ignition and headers. Lift is .505 on the intake, .516 on the exhaust, with 224 degrees on the intake, 232 degrees on the exhaust. The cam has 108-degree lobe centers. The other change was that we went back to the Streetmaster, using the same carburetor jetting as in test No. 5. However, the torque characteristics of the engine changed significantly. Maximum torque of 333 lbs.-ft. @ 4000 rpm moved the peak output well up the rpm range, and the BSFC moved up accordingly to .518. However, the

engine output climbed to 282 horsepower @ 4500 rpm (a jump of 31 horsepower over the stock cam/ Streetmaster combo) and continued to a maximum of 302 @ 5000. We could have buzzed it up a little tighter, but "Hook" chickened out, and we were never able to see what the ol' Henry could really do.

TEST NO. 8:
This run featured two basic changes to the 351, in the hope of coming up with a good low- to mid-range combination. First we installed Crane's HT-288-2-NC hydraulic cam (encompassing 288 degrees duration on the intakes, 298 degrees duration on the exhausts, .496-inch lift on the intakes, .517-inch lift on the exhausts with 112-degree lobe centers) that was said to provide good, low-end torque. The second change was to reinstall the SP2P intake/Holley 600 with stock jetting. As you can see, the swap proved bountiful. The torque curve picked up considerably, to 3500, and provided a maximum of 337 lbs.-ft. @ 3000 rpm and a BSFC of .460 at the same rpm range. Horsepower was 258 @ 5000 rpm.

TEST NO. 9:
The final test was made to see if extending the header pipes and collector an additional 3 inches would result in an increase of torque. At 3000, we picked up 6 more lbs.-ft. (343), while the BSFC stood at .457. Obviously, the change in length improved the torque in the 2700-3000-rpm range while dropping the BSFC. Horsepower at 4500 rpm was 263.

Obviously, we could have played with various combinations until we wore out either Holly's hound or my typewriter. However, Kurt Hooker wanted to know what combination Holly wanted before they returned the 351 to the Ranchero. Jim McFarland's answer was significant: "Let Holly look at these dyno figures; then let him decide!" **HR**

The 351 Cleveland

Ford's old standby still has lots of life

Over the years, Ford's 351 Cleveland engine has been the most popular of the so-called mid-sized engines among Ford high-performance enthusiasts. Though outnumbered by the ubiquitous Chevy small-block, the 351 Cleveland has more than held its own both in competition and on the street. This engine is still the favorite contender for the high-performance treatment among Ford-ophiles. It's available, there's an abundance of go-fast parts for it, and there's been substantial development of its potential.

Although two-bolt-main versions of the 351 Cleveland have been successfully modified, the four-bolt-main block is so common, it makes more sense to use it and be on the safe side. That's the heart of this particular buildup, an engine that puts out impressive horsepower without giving up reliability and without being prohibitively expensive. The parts that were used, both OEM and aftermarket, are readily available, and the techniques involved in putting them together are not beyond the expertise of most engine builders.

1. Mike Cook align hones the block after sonic check and cleanup. This is preferable to align boring because it doesn't change the distance between the crank and cam centers.

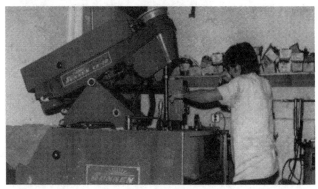
2. Sunnen power hone used No. 280 grit stone to produce a No. 625 finish. A torque plate was used to simulate head distortion.

Engine Block

The first thing to do when preparing your 351 Cleveland block is to have it hot-tanked, acid stripped and Magnafluxed. The acid stripping is recommended so that rust deposits don't fool the sonic testing machine into thinking there's more cylinder wall than there actually is.

Once the block is checked out and thoroughly cleaned, a set of FPP (Ford Power Parts) stainless steel screw-in water plugs is installed using a 1⅛-inch M.P.T. cutter to tap the block. It is then power-honed on a Sunnen CK-10 machine with a McCord No. 6850 head gasket and a torque plate to prevent distortion. The pistons chosen for this engine were TRWs with 10.5:1 compression. These call for a .004 cylinder wall clearance, which was obtained by using a 280 grit stone to achieve the 625 finish. The block was also line-honed before one piston and rod was mocked-up onto the crank to check the deck height in all four corners.

The lowest corner of each deck surface was used as a reference to take a .020 cut to give a final deck height of .010. The reason that the lowest is used is because any block can vary as much as 0.30 inch side to side and front to back in deck height. After the completion of block machining, it is cleaned with soap and water, washed in lacquer thinner and painted on the inside with Glyphthol varnish. This aids the flow of oil and also seals in any microscopic particles that might have escaped the cleaning process.

Crankshaft

The stock 351 Cleveland cast-iron crankshaft is used in this engine. It too

3. TRW 10.5:1 pistons and wrist pins were used with ceramic rings and dual Spirolox.

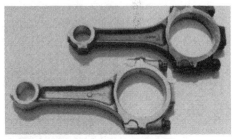
4. Ford Power Parts' new Cleveland Capscrew rods use the same capscrews as 427 Ford.

5. The difference between old rod (top) and new one is apparent.

6. Floating pin is preferred over pressed pin. Spirolox retainer shown.

7. N.P.T. cutter was used to tap threads for FPP stainless steel water plugs, which were installed using liquid Teflon to prevent leakage.

9. Crane F-246 solid-lifter cam has lift of .570-.590 and duration (at .050 lift) of 246-256 degrees. It's a perfect cam for street operation.

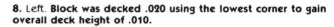

8. Left. Block was decked .020 using the lowest corner to gain overall deck height of .010.

12. Exhaust is undercut 45 degrees and unshrouded to aid flow.

13. Exhaust port work is extensive, includes radiusing the seats.

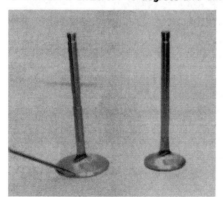

17. Valves were back-cut at 45 degrees, and an additional 22-degree cut was taken to create a smooth radius from stem to seat.

18. Valve seat runout was held to .0005.

19. Exhaust seat was narrowed to a width of .080 to help flow.

is Magnafluxed, though a powder Mag is insufficient. A wet Mag check with a blacklight will show any cracks, however. Even though most used cranks will probably check out to standard size, grinding and micropolishing is recommended. After grinding the crankshaft, the oil holes are chamfered and micropolished.

The next step is to heat treat the crank for added strength. This leaves a residue on the crank journals that micropolishing will remove. Check the crank for straightness by laying it in the block, using well-oiled bearings, and bolting the front and rear main caps on

snugly. A dial indicator is placed on the center journal, and the crank is turned slowly. A good, straight crankshaft should have less than .0005 runout. If it has more, it should be professionally straightened.

Connecting Rods

The rods chosen for this engine are the new FPP Capscrew Clevelands as developed by Ron Miller of Ford Power Parts. They're stock rods modified to accept 7/16x20-inch, 180,000 psi tensile-strength capscrew bolts, which are identical to the aftermarket bolts used on 427 Ford rods. These rods are

completely reconditioned from a 3/8-inch nut-and-bolt setup to a 7/16-inch capscrew.

Initially, the stock 351 Cleveland rods are checked for cracks and flaws, then the beams are polished and shot-peened. Next, Miller drills and taps the rods (for aligning the dowels) using a mill and rod fixture that holds the rod in perfect alignment. The rods are torqued to 75 ft.-pounds. The big end is resized, and the small end is bushed (using thick bushings) to equalize center-to-center dimensions. The top end of the rod is then drilled with an oiling hole for the wrist pin and honed for fit.

10. Heads were cut a total of .037 to match block and reduce combustion chamber volume to the desired 63.4 ccs.

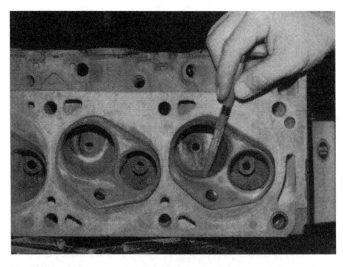

11. Airflow is increased by a 45-degree undercut of the seat.

14. Head modifications increased flow by five cfm.

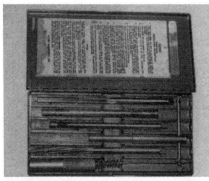

15. Manley Valve Guide kit was used to hone bronze guides.

16. Bronze guides are carefully installed before honing.

20. Manley Valve Guide Tool can be seen between seat-measuring calipers.

21. Crane triple springs were installed with 125 pounds of pressure with the valves closed.

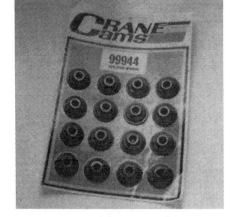

22. Crane steel retainers were chosen over aluminum for reliability.

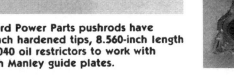

24. Ford Power Parts pushrods have two-inch hardened tips, 8.560-inch length and .040 oil restrictors to work with ⅜-inch Manley guide plates.

23. Left. Moroso heavy-duty rocker studs have extra large radius to withstand high spring pressures.

25. Polished Hall Pantera manifold was matched to intake ports.

26. Inglese installed a set of his reverse mounting plates so that all the Webers run in same direction for more efficient linkage geometry.

27. Inglese prepared Weber 48 IDAs using his needle-and-seat assembly to double fuel flow pressure to nine pounds. Stock 37mm chokes were replaced with 45mm units, and lower rpm and accelerator pump circuits were modified to operate under 3000 rpm.

30. Block was carefully deburred before diligent cleaning and painting.

31. Bearings were measured before installation to make sure they met standards.

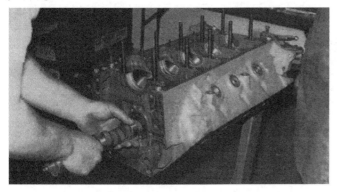

35. Cam bearing clearances (.001-.003) are checked by measuring the inside diameter of the cam bearings and subtracting the outside diameter of the cam bearing journals.

36. After the block is thoroughly cleaned, crank is laid in well-oiled bearings, and the main caps are installed and torqued.

If you build your engine using stock 351 Cleveland rods, Miller recommends full-floating pins. They create less friction and allow easier assembly, while correcting rod lengths. The center-to-center length might vary considerably. A full-floating pin also eliminates the possibility of a pressed pin coming loose and destroying a cylinder wall.

With the TRW flat-top pistons, the pin must be shortened, and the grooves for the pin must be machined for either single or double Spirolox. In this engine, double Spirolox are used. With 12:1 pistons (TRW L2348F with closed chamber heads, or L2408F with open chamber heads), the grooves are already cut and the pins are shortened. However, these pistons come with Tru-Arc snap rings, which occasionally pop out. Consequently, it's best to use Spirolox retainers even though they cost about a dollar each. Also, they should never be reused.

Balancing

The 351 Cleveland's components should be dynamically balanced even if only stock pieces have been used. The factory balance job can be off as much as 11 grams per part and still pass inspection. A good balancing shop can reduce the tolerances to less than a half-gram.

You should have the reciprocating assembly balanced only after all clearances have been checked. For example, piston-to-valve clearance is sufficient at .100 on the intake and .120 on the exhaust. To attain these clearances, it may be necessary to grind some metal off the pistons, something you don't want to do after balancing.

Heads

The heads were decked .010 to match the block and then prepared to a street finish by Chris Kaufman of

28. Finished Weber setup has black carb bodies, chrome bolts, gold-plated screens and five-inch velocity stacks.

29. Moroso Oil Restrictor kit (part No. 2205) increases supply of oil to main bearings.

32,33,34. Before crank installation, the main bearings were torqued to 105 ft.-lbs. and checked with micrometer. The width of the bearings is then subtracted, and the result, when compared against the crank journal diameter, reveals the actual clearance.

37. Crank is carefully levered back and forth to check end-play at thrust bearing.

38. End play of .005 is acceptable. (All high-stress bolts—mains, rods and heads—were torqued in increments of 20 ft.-lbs.)

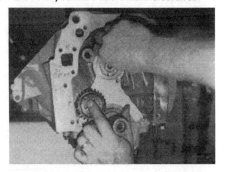

39. An important step in the installation of the Milodon gear drive (part No. 14200) is drilling the lower holes into the Cleveland block. A backlash of .002-.003 is most critical.

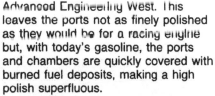

Advanced Engineering West. This leaves the ports not as finely polished as they would be for a racing engine but, with today's gasoline, the ports and chambers are quickly covered with burned fuel deposits, making a high polish superfluous.

If you plan on doing your own head work, use a Dumore high-speed grinder with a Merit abrasive polishing stone. A good head fixture is the secret to achieving a successful port job, since it lets you get into hard-to-reach areas with control.

The head work begins with a blending of the 45-degree angle in the valve

40. After the cam has been degreed-in (1½ degree advanced), the vernier cam gear is installed in its final location and torqued to 25 ft.-lbs. A mock-up rod and piston assembly is installed in the number one cylinder, and a complete head is bolted on. Valves are set at zero lash to determine piston-to-valve clearance, which should be roughly .100 on the intakes and .120 on the exhausts.

42. Be careful not to stretch the Spirolox when installing wrist pins, and make sure they are properly seated in their grooves.

41. Left. Fish scale is used to check oil ring tangential tension. Oil the cylinder walls and attach the scale to the piston. Stock tension should be 25-30 pounds, and 8-10 pounds for racing.

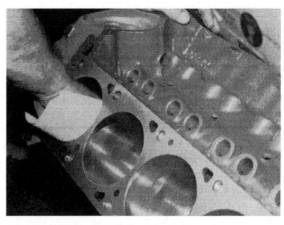

43. Before assembly, final cleaning is critical. Absorbent paper with ATF (it has a high-detergent rate) is used initially, followed with Pennzoil or CRC cleaner and a paper towel.

46. Mark rod/cap assemblies using machinists blue so that they're not inadvertantly mismatched. Use oil and Permatex grey anti-seize when installing rod bolts.

47. With all the rods and pistons in place, use dual feeler gauges to square the rods against each other. The cap bolts are torqued to 60 ft.-lbs. in 20 ft.-lb. increments. Then they're pulled smoothly up to 75 ft.-lbs. If the rod bolts squeak, they need more assembly lube.

48. Use ample assembly lube when installing Crane lifters in the block.

50. Heads are torqued in same sequence as all 10-bolt Ford heads, starting with middle-upper bolt to middle-lower, and working in that pattern from side to side. Torque begins at 30 ft.-lbs., going up in 20 ft.-lb. increments to 70 and 85 ft.-lbs. The rate is then increased to 100 ft.-lbs. for final torquing. The Moroso screw-in valve studs are torqued to 75 ft.-lbs.

51. New FPP pushrods have two-inch hardened ends with .040 oil restrictors. Anti-seize was used on each pushrod end to prevent initial start-up galling.

52. Crane roller rockers were adjusted with 9/16-inch wrench and .026 feeler gauge. Bottom end torque can be increased by setting clearances a few thousandths looser; whereas tightening the lash helps on the top end.

seats to unshroud the intake and exhaust. The combustion chambers are polished, including radiusing the rough seats for a smooth transition in the port-to-valve area. Care must be taken not to eat up the valve seats while polishing.

The exhaust port area requires the most attention; it must be unshrouded to reduce the radius around which the burned gases flow. This lets the gases pass more smoothly and increases their velocity. Still, the exhaust ports of the 351 Cleveland are the worst aspect

of the head's design. Ideally, they should be reconfigured to match the high-port exhaust plate heads used by Pro Stock racers. Or, you can use the new Ford SVO high-port aluminum heads (Ford part No. M-6049-83), but these are a bit exotic for street use. However, a careful port job like Chris Kaufman's can add five cfm over a stock head on the flow bench.

A Manley Valve Guide kit was used to install bronze valve guides, which were honed to the required .002-0025 stem clearances. The seats were

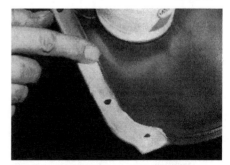

55. To avoid leakage, a lot of white grease is applied to the oil pan rail before installation.

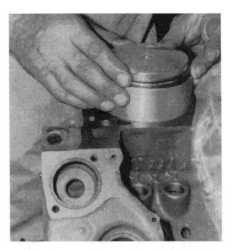

44. A light film of 10-weight Sta-Lube is applied to rings and pistons before assembly.

45. FPP tapered-ring compressor is used for installation along with thin oil such as Sta-Lube, Wesson or a mineral oil. Heavy oil will hamper ring break-in.

49. Completed heads have Manley valves and guide plates, Crane roller rockers and springs and FPP valve cover stud kit. Block and head surfaces were cleaned with lacquer thinner before assembly.

Bottom End

53. FPP blueprinted high-volume oil pump and Moroso pickup are installed with 25 ft.-lbs. of torque. Don't forget to install the FPP oil pump drive (part No. 1306) before installing the distributor.

54. Generous amount of Ford contact cement is used on the engine and gaskets to keep gasket from walking when the oil pan is torqued down.

56. When bolting a pan down, start from the center bolt holes and alternately work your way toward the front and back of the pan. Tighten the small ¼-inch pan studs seven-nine ft.-lbs. and torque the ⁵⁄₁₆-inch end studs nine-11 ft.-lbs.

CLEVELAND 351 BUILDUP PARTS LIST

Engine Block—FFP used '71 Boss 351 Cleveland, four-bolt mains

PART	PART NUMBER
Crank—FFP, '71 Cleveland	4524 HT
Bearings—TRW	MS3010+10
Rods—FPP Capscrew	
Cleveland	2560
Rod Bearings—TRW	CB927P-10
Main Bearings—TRW	MF3010P-10
Pistons—TRW	L2379F+30
Rings—TRW Moly	T9117+35
Spirolox—TRW	LR211
Cam—Crane F246	521211
Cam Bearings—Durabond	F-26
Screw-In Freeze Plugs—FPP	no part No. assigned
Main Stud Kit—FPP	3203
Oil Pump—FPP	1322BP-HP
Oil Pump Drive—FPP	1306
Oil Pump Stud Kit—FPP	3335
Oil Pan Stud Kit—FPP	3301
Oil Pan—Moroso	2056
Oil Pickup—Moroso	2455
Oil Restrictor Kit—Moroso	2205
Gear Drive—B&M/Milodon	14200
Water Pump—Weiand aluminum	8209
Flywheel—McLeod	463-203
Gaskets—Mr. Gasket, Rear	
Main	1966
Oil Pan	293

HEADS

'71 Boss 351 Cleveland by Chris Kaufman & Greg Foreman

Valves—Manley intake	11800
exhaust	11805
Head Studs—Moroso	6782
Guide Plates—Manley	42156
Lifters—Crane	99257
Rockers—Crane	27750
Valve Springs—Crane	99886
Retainers—Crane ¹¹⁄₃₂ inch	99944
Valve Seals—Crane	99820
Valve Locks—Crane	99041
Pushrods—FPP—³⁄₈ × 8.560 inch	1655
Valve Cover Stud Kit—FPP	3320
Valve Cover Gaskets—Mr. Gasket	274
Head Gaskets—McCord	6850
Intake Gaskets—Mr. Gasket	214
Valve Covers—Ford Motorsport	M-6582-A341

INTAKE MANIFOLDS

Holley Strip Dominator	300-13
Hall Pantera Weber intake	PN1001

CARBURETION

Inglese Stage III IDA Weber carburetors with five-inch chrome velocity stacks
Holley 850 Dominator—Old-style

with hand choke	4781
Four-point idle with no choke	8162

IGNITION

Distributor—Accel II modified

with an Allison XR-700 kit	37202T
Coil—Allison	PS20
Wires—Allison	PS1105
Spark Plugs—Autolite	AF32

Engine Front Assembly

57. Cleveland front cover and stock Ford gasket are sandwiched between Weiand aluminum water pump (part No. 8209), which is bolted on using FPP 5/16-inch stud kit.

Valve Covers

60. Ford Motorsport finned aluminum valve covers required the removal of internal oil baffles to clear Crane rollers.

63. Final assembly included installation of Allison plug wires, Autolite AF22 spark plugs, Cleveland dip stick tube, fuel pump block-off plate and other related hardware.

ground to a 45-degree angle to match the valve faces. Seat runout was checked and corrected to a tolerance of .0005. The top valve cut (22 degrees) was just "kissed" to allow blending the chamber into the valve seat. At the bottom, a cut angle of 67.5 degrees was used to narrow the valve seat to the desired width of .050-inch on the intake and .080-inch on the exhaust. The bottom cut was then blended into the throat area of each valve. After the seats were finished, the valves were ground with 45-degree face angles to ensure proper concentricity. The valves were also cut to the tuliped area to blend with the seat.

After they were mocked up and the chambers measured, it was necessary to mill the heads .027 to reduce the chamber volume from 67.8 ccs to the desired 63.4 ccs.

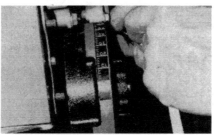

58. After degreeing-in, stock Ford damper was found to be off 12 degrees, making installation of Mr. Gasket timing tape necessary. Make sure damper is absolutely clean so tape will stick.

61. Accel Racing II distributor was machined out to accept Allison XR-700 electronic conversion kit, gaining 12 degrees at 2800 rpm, with the curve starting at 950 rpm. This allows 24 degrees at the crank, 30-40-degree total lead.

64. Gary Griggs fabricated a set of Cyclone A-Rs from 1¾-inch tubing. Anti-Reversion method reduces tie intensity of any gas pressure pulse coming back up the pipe, without hindering the flow.

Intake and Carburetion

Two induction combinations were tried on this engine: a practical and comparatively inexpensive carburetor setup, which used a Holley 850 Dominator and an exotic Weber setup.

The Holley was mounted on a Holley Strip Dominator manifold, while the Weber was modified and fitted to a Hall Pantera manifold by Jim Inglese. He disassembled the bodies and replaced the needle-and-seat assemblies, choke sleeves and low rpm and idle circuits. He also painted and detailed the carbs.

Dyno testing, using Cyclone headers, produced a high of 441 horsepower with the Weber and 426 with the Holley. Impressive results were gained more by diligent and intelligent engine building than by vast expenditures of money and the use of custom-made parts. ●

Intake Manifold Installation

59. White grease was used to hold gaskets in place, while either the Hall Pantera or Holley Dominator manifolds were bolted on using chromemoly washers and 28 ft.-lbs. of torque.

62. Before installing distributor, make sure to insert special chromemoly FPP oil pump drive.

65. With the Webers installed, the engine went through a series of runs up to 5500 rpm. An initial pull with street headers yielded a best of 427 hp at 408 ft.-lbs. Following the installation of a set of Feuling/Cyclone A-Rs, the horsepower rose to 441 and torque to 421.

CONTRIBUTORS

Ford Power Parts
14504 S. Carmenita Unit C
Norwalk, CA 90650

Advanced Engineering West
12418½ Benedict Ave.
Downey, CA 90242

Cook's Auto Parts & Service
24210 S. Avalon Blvd.
Carson, CA 90745

Feuling Engineering
Bldg. 10, Chino Airport
Chino, CA 91710

Hall Pantera
9210½ Alondra Blvd.
Bellflower, CA 90706

Inglese
11 Tipping Dr.
Branford, CT 06405

Affordable Ford performance

MODIFYING THE
FORD 351 CLEVELAND
TO DELIVER AN HONEST
600 HP AT 9500 RPM
By Marlan Davis

The Ford 351 Cleveland can produce more horsepower per cubic inch with carburetors on gasoline than any other American motor. The canted valve head design allows huge diameter valves for its displacement size, and with proper head work, especially on the exhaust side, the Cleveland has proven to be virtually unbeatable—when not forced by various sanctioning bodies to carry extra weight. But since it doesn't come stamped with a "bow tie," parts availability tends to be some-what limited, and those parts that can be found are usually more expensive than other "Brand X" pieces.

One man who has persevered and overcome this problem is Mark Degroff, general manager at Valley Head Service, 19340 Londelius St., Northridge, California 91324, (213) 993-7000. When he's not machining heads or building engines for customers, Mark's out racing a C/Modified Production '65 Mustang (see HOT ROD, August '79) with partner Doug Wright.

For the 3400-pound car to run consistent 10 teens at 135 mph (Mark has gone as quick as 10.03) in the 9.7-pound/cubic-inch C/MP class, requires a 357-inch (.030-over 351) Cleveland that puts out an honest 600 hp at 9500 rpm, that's backed by a 3.25 low gear Doug Nash 5-speed and 6.50-geared Dana rearend. That kind of rpm requires an engine nearly as radical as a Pro Stock motor, yet Mark feels his combination could be duplicated for around $6000, assuming the builder does all the work

Affordable performance

(except for major machining and headwork). However, a radical high-output motor such as this one does require frequent major maintenance: The ring seal goes away after about 25 runs and a valve job is necessary after 50. After every race, the engine is torn down and inspected.

BLOCK PREP

Mark begins with a used 4-bolt-main Cleveland block, which came stock on the '71 Boss 351. A few other passenger blocks, including some from Mercury stationwagons, have also been known to turn up with 4-bolt-mains. Two-bolt-main blocks have enough meat to add the extra bolt holes, but aftermarket caps would have to be used since Ford doesn't sell new caps without an engine. Used blocks are preferable to

Moroso restrictor kit is installed to prevent oil starving mains. Galleys feeding into No. 5 main saddle (circled) are most important. Middle hole goes to cam and is tapped to receive 5/16 coarse thread restrictor. Left-hand hole is left alone as it feeds oil from pump via passenger-side lifter galley to this bearing. Hole on right sends oil from bearing to driver-side lifter galley; it's restricted with ⅜ coarse plug. Small galleys in saddle Nos. 2-4 that feed oil to cam are tapped for ¼-inch-20 .040 restrictor plugs (arrows). No. 1 hole is left alone; since main oil galley passage from filter and cam passage criss-cross underneath main web, plugging it would only restrict oil to bearing.

new ones because their cylinder walls have already shifted as much as they're going to.

Only three machining operations are required to prepare the block for racing—align boring, cylinder wall honing and deck surfacing. According to Mark, "We don't strive for any particular deck height on the block because we individually adjust the piston by machining it to achieve a nominal zero deck with the head gasket installed." Normally only a .005-inch surfacing cut is taken, and the block is left as tall as possible.

Standard Moroso small-block Chevy windage screen is modified for use on Cleveland by bending to semi-circular configuration and trimming to fit crank cavity, as shown. Original modified screen ended at No. 4 saddle, but rod failure has since sliced it off. Block is tapped on outside edge for ¼-inch-20 bolts that retain homemade sheetmetal brackets.

Standard TRW high-volume oil pump is used with normal passenger-car pickup brazed onto screen as insurance against factory weld breaking. Other end is securely fastened into pump body with ⅛-inch pin replacing the factory screw-in method. Pin is peened on both ends to achieve tight seal and prevent minute vacuum leaks which can aerate oil as it's sucked through blades. Ears are welded onto screen so in event of oil pan failure, pump-to-pan clearance will still be retained and oil starvation prevented. Pump driveshaft is bulletproof steel piece from Pro-Stock Engineering, Inc., 16102 Orange Ave., Paramount, CA 90723.

Cylinder overbores have ranged from as little as .020 to as large as .060 (his current 351 is .030 over), and are done using a torque plate to simulate cylinder head bolt distortion. Cylinder walls are finished as smooth as possible on the Sunnen CK-10 honing machine. Mark starts with a 625 stone (approximately 400-grit), progressing to an 820 (about 600-grit). Then a special ultra-fine C3003 800-grit stone is used for the final .0002-inch.

OILING

Unlike some other Cleveland engine builders, Mark does not perform any radical oiling system mods. A simple Moroso oil restrictor kit is used to limit oil flow to the driver-side lifter galley and cam journals (see photo). All you have to do is tap the holes and put in the Allen screws, which come predrilled to the correct restrictor size.

Other key oil system ingredients include a TRW high-volume oil pump, TRW fully grooved main bearings and Crane roller lifters featuring a very small waist that allows oil to flow more easily past it. This feature is desirable since the Cleveland feeds the rear main bearing through the passenger-side lifter galley.

RECIPROCATING ASSEMBLY

Ford never offered a forged crank for the Cleveland, but Mark has found the stock cast-iron unit, as reworked by Velasco, to be more than adequate. The crank is cross-drilled for 360-degree oiling and Tufftrided. To

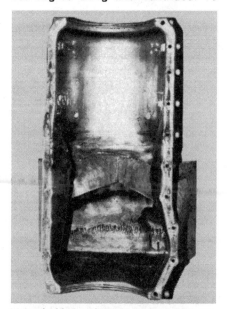

Instead of being deepened, stock 351 pan was widened to increase capacity to nine quarts (with filter) from stock five. This allows stock length pickup to be used and helps ground clearance. (As seen from this pan's slightly bulged-in sides caused by post-wheelstand letdown you can't have enough!)

better cut through the oil at high rpm, the counterweights are streamlined or "knife-edged." On cars that see a broad rpm range, such as Mark's 5-speed Modified Mustang, this mod is reportedly worth as much as 30 hp and 2 mph on the top end. Cars that experience little rpm fluctuation—such as a Powerglide-equipped Econo dragster—do not seem to benefit all that much.

The crank's rod throws are cut down from the stock 2.311-inch to the Chevy small-block's 2.1-inch diameter. Bearing speed is thereby slowed, which translates to more rpm capability and less chance of spinning a rod bearing. What's more, it's now easy to stroke the crank as much as .400-inch up or down from stock, since the journals are being cut anyway. Mark is currently running a longer-than-stock 6.1-inch aluminum Super Rod, which he prefers because it's the lightest aluminum connecting rod on the market, yet is still strong enough to last about 80 runs. With the stock stroke crank in his present engine, the "ideal" 1.8:1 rod/stroke ratio is achieved. Although a shorter stroke would allow more rpm, the heads seem to feed best on a motor displacing around 350 inches.

For pistons Mark uses a gas-ported Venolia Pro Stock racing unit run with .007 cylinder wall clearance. The gas porting promotes better high rpm sealing in conjunction with the spe-

cial Sealed Power ring set, consisting of a .043-inch plasma moly top and 1/16 tapered face cast-iron second (gapped at .014 and .012, respectively), along with a special SS50U ⅛ low-tension chrome-faced stainless-steel oil ring. Mark also feels the Venolia dome configuration offers good flame propagation, while the pistons' ground-round skirt is easy on the cylinder walls. As it's among the thinnest of American engines, the Cleveland's walls tend to crack when ex-

Crank is internally balanced with Mallory heavy metal in front (shown, see arrows) and rear counterweights, reducing load and strain on No. 1 bearing caused from supporting very heavy counterweighted dampener located two or three inches in front of it. To aid high-rpm stability, engine is actually overbalanced 52 percent. Counterweights are knife-edged to cut through oil better at high rpm. Studs are used on inside of 4-bolt-main bearing caps since stock Ford bolts aren't strong enough to withstand 100 ft./lbs. of torque called for in racing use. They're more than adequate for outside holes, where only 45 ft./lbs. is needed. Rod and main bearings run .0025-.003-inch clearance. Thrust clearance is .005-.008-inch.

posed to the more common slipper-type skirt.

Each piston is recontoured by hand all the way around so it fits the combustion chamber as closely as possible when the motor is first assembled. As temperature and rpm increase, the dome actually gets so close to the cylinder head in certain areas that the carbon buildup is brushed off (see photo). As Mark says, "It's one way of verifying the piston is as close as it can possibly get!" So far, that comes out to .050 piston-to-valve clearance on the intakes and .080 on the exhaust. More clearance is required on the exhaust side because the piston is chasing the closing valve and would hit it if the valve momentarily floated.

As the life of the engine progresses and the connecting rods continue to stretch and take a set, a file is periodically taken to the piston's quench area where it's hitting hardest. Then .003-.004-inch of stock is taken off, enabling the motor to get another 15-20 runs in before the procedure has to be repeated.

A relatively large rod side clearance of .050-inch is run to avoid any restriction on total oil flow through the bottom end. Although this always keeps the bearings cool, such large clearances may throw additional oil on the cylinder walls. However, the gas-ported pistons and special ring

Venolia pistons are retained on Super Rods by standard Venolia 66-gram, 2.5-inch-diameter non-tapered, thinwall wrist pins held in place by dual Spirolocks on each end. Special Sealed Power ring set designed for gas-ported pistons is used. Domes are smoothed and recontoured by hand to fit chamber as closely as possible, giving aproximate 14:1 compression ratio. Fit is so tight that carbon is actually brushed off by chamber roof (note light spots on dark carbon-covered used piston). Fully grooved TRW MS-3010B main bearings fit in stock Ford caps, aid oiling. Caps are retained by stock Ford ⅜-inch bolts in outside holes and Automotive Racing Products ½-inch chrome moly screw-in studs with hardened nuts and washers. Since rod journals have been cut down to 2.1-inch Chevy size, TRW 350 Chevy rod bearings (part No. CB-824P), predrilled for retaining dowel pin, are used.

Since engine is internally balanced, factory counterweight on stock balancer (bottom) is machined out. Dampener outer portion has reputation for separating from rubber layer, so holes are drilled and tapped opposite each other (arrows) for bolts that act like dowel pins to keep outer rim indexed while allowing rubber to flex and retain its dampening effect.

Affordable performance

combo seem well up to handling it.

One other trick Mark performs on the bottom end is to replace the stock rope-type rear main seals with Fel-Pro BS40042 rubber pieces. This is done because the stock seals put excessive drag on the crank.

CAMSHAFT AND VALVETRAIN

The cam used is a Crower roller grind (part No. S-0291) ground on

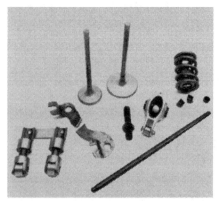

Bulletproof pieces are required to handle .700 lift cam at over 9500 rpm. Crane No. 52718 roller lifters push cut-down TRW chrome moly big-block Chevy ⅜-inch pushrods. Then 1.625 o.d. Crower Vascojet springs (part No. 68555-1), capped with titanium retainers held in place by 10-degree split locks (part No. 86068), are adjusted by hardened stainless-steel shims to installed height of 1.950 inches, giving 200 pounds of seat pressure (750 open). Standard 1.73:1 Norris big-block Chevy rocker arms are used on Automotive Racing Products chrome moly rocker arm studs (part No. RRS1-7/16). Standard size Del West 11/32-inch stem titanium valves (2.19 intake/1.70 exhaust) are protected from wear caused by rocker arms with Competition Cams lash cap. Guideplates are modified Chevy rat parts.

Stock Chevy ⅜-inch pushrod guideplate (part No. 3860038) (top) is cut in half and bent slightly on ends for use in Mark's Cleveland; necessary because distance between 351's stud centerline and pushrod is less than on Chevy. It's practically a bolt-on operation—just install on head, bend, index for proper relationship to pushrod and torque down stud.

109-degree lobe centers with 71 degrees of overlap and .785/.787 lift and 328/332-degree duration on the intakes and exhaust, respectively. Mark gave Crower all the pertinent information on the engine, drivetrain, chassis and intended application, along with complete data on head flow rates at varying valve lifts, and they did the rest. Says Mark, "It's the best cam I've ever run." If he could, he'd use a rev kit with it, except that no one offers such a setup for the Cleveland.

A variety of different manufacturers parts are used to complete the valvetrain (see photo). Many are modified from parts originally developed for the big-block Chevy, which has similarly designed cylinder heads with canted valves and independent stud-mounted rocker arms. Even the two engines' valvestem heights are within .025 of each other; the face diameter of the intake valves (2.19 inches) is exacly the same. Mark has found a

Overall distance on this Norris big-block Chevy rocker arm between trunion (A) and roller (B) is .020-inch longer than on Ford piece. With radical rocker arm movement generated by high-lift cam, added length means roller will be closer to center of valve stem, resulting in less wear.

Pro-Stock Engineering's ProDex timing chain and indexed gearset permits easy changes of cam timing. Cam is normally run straight up, but at times is retarded as much as 2 degrees to ensure proper relationship to piston if dome or rod stroke is slightly off. Occasionally cam is advanced 1 degree to compensate for chain stretch. Object is to "run cam as close as possible to what Crower recommends."

part ostensibly made for a "big-block Chevy" is usually cheaper than one "special ordered" for a "351 Cleveland."

Since the two motors aren't exactly the same, some mods are required when using certain Chevy parts. For example, the TRW big-block Chevy ⅜-inch-diameter pushrods are almost ¾-inch too long (due to the rat's higher deck), so the pressed-in tip on the guideplate end is removed in a lathe, the pushrod is shortened, and the tip is reinstalled under one-ton pressure. This will provide an inexpensive—yet effective—Cleveland-style unit. Guideplates can also be modified from Chevy parts, as shown in the photos.

CYLINDER HEADS & INDUCTION

The heads Mark likes to use are (in order of desirability) the Boss 302, Boss 351 and 351-4V closed chamber. Boss 302 heads can be adapted

Closed chamber head (left) is preferred over open chamber version since it's easier to get compression up.

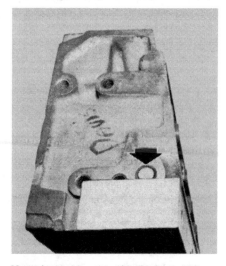

Most desired head is '69-'70 Boss 302 because it can achieve better exhaust port layout. Unlike Cleveland head, it has a cast-in smog device hole (arrow). A 7/16 hardened steel shaft can be inserted in this hole, allowing porter to cut higher into exhaust port roof than on Cleveland. Result is a better flowing port.

Affordable performance

to fit the Cleveland with minor mods, and their design allows more work to be done in the exhaust port area than in the other two. These heads, as well as those of the Boss 351, are machined for screw-in rocker arm studs and pushrod guideplates, unlike the 351-4V heads (although they can be modified to accept them). Closed chamber 4V heads are preferred over late-model, open chamber smog heads because it's easier to get the desired 14:1 compression with the former. Of course, 2V heads of any year are totally undesirable for drag racing.

Whichever head is used should be surfaced to achieve a 55cc combustion chamber. Typically, this requires a .060 cut; angle-milling is unnecessary since there's more than enough meat on the heads.

All heads receive a full competition port and polish. The ends of the stock exhaust ports are cut off and replaced with a raised aluminum plate, a mod which is relatively straightforward nowadays. The intake port is thoroughly hogged out and streamlined around the valve. Mark cuts as high as he can into the port roof, trying to straighten it all the way

from the valve guide as far up the Edelbrock tunnel ram as possible. The valves get a special Valley Head Service valve job and are installed in special K-Line silicone-bronze .015-inch-diameter thinwall valve guides, which are sealed with Perfect Circle Teflon pieces that fit inside the Crower valvespring.

Finally, the heads are O-ringed to complement a special McCord .050-inch compressed thickness composition head gasket (part No. 6850). With the O-ringing and this gasket, the heads need only 80 ft./lbs. of torque to seal them (compared to the recommended stock figure of 100-125 pounds). Mark feels that lower bolt torque causes less distortion of the heads, leading to much better valve sealing.

The motor is topped off by two Holley 650 double-pumpers (Model 4150, List 0-4777). Mark prefers these carburetors over the huge 1050/1150-cfm 4500 Dominators because the larger carb doesn't seem to respond as well as the 650 to the sudden drastic rpm changes experienced in a manually shifted car. Since the Edelbrock UR-19 tunnel ram is designed for the 4500, adapter plates had to be fabricated. The smaller size 4150 carb provides additional distributor clearance, so the carbs can be moved further forward than the 4500 on the intake for optimum positioning directly over the manifold plenum, thus giving fuel a

straighter shot into the ports.

The carbs are run surprisingly stock: Naturally, jetting varies, depending on track and atmospheric conditions. The jets are staggered to compensate for rich and lean cylinders. No power valves are used. The air horn is milled off for better air flow—since the choke's been done away with it's redundant anyway. To prevent loading up at idle, or flooding the engine with an overly rich charge when mashing the brakes after a burnout, the idle metering circuit is restricted with .017-inch-diameter wire.

The combination, when properly maintained, consistently provides Mark with afFORDable performance. Why not try some of his better ideas?   **HR**

Cleveland head *(front)* doesn't have rear water crossover passage like Boss 302 does. To use Boss 302 heads on Cleveland block, this water passage must be blocked off.

OPERATING AND TUNING DATA

Fuel:	Daeco 105-octane, ½-inch fuel line, Holley electric pump
Fuel Pressure:	8 pounds with dual pressure regulators
Oil:	Valvoline 20W-50 racing
Oil Filter:	Fram
Oil Pressure:	60 psi (average)
Thermostat:	None (block run through quarter dry)
Normal Operating Temperature:	180 degrees off line; boils over in lights
Ignition Timing:	40 degrees total, fully advanced at idle
Spark Plugs:	Autolite AF-701 racing
Plug Gap:	.040-inch
Valve Lash:	Intake—.026-inch (hot), .024-inch (cold) Exhaust—.028-inch (hot), .026 (cold)
Carb Jetting:	Stagger-jetted, 74 average
Power Valves:	None
Accelerator Pump Squirter Diameter:	.035-inch
Headers:	Home-built using Hooker kit: 2¼-inch-diameter primaries, 24 inches long; 4-inch-diameter collector, 10 inches long, dictated by chassis considerations

Here is what completed engine looks like, topped by 650 Holley double-pumpers minus choke and airhorn. Original photo-electric-triggered Accel BEI lights spark. Water pump is rare Ford aluminum muscle part piece (part No. DOZX-8505-A). No water actually circulates through block during run; pump is electrically actuated by Mr. Gasket water pump drive kit (part No. 4333) and circulates cool water from radiator through block on return road. Need to add water manually is eliminated, except in event of boilover.

HOW-TO: **351 CLEVELAND V-8 TUNE-UP**

Ford refers to the "Cleveland" engine design as the "335" series, which includes displacements of 351 cu. ins. and 400 cu. ins. The 351C (for Cleveland) was introduced in 1970, and its bigger brother came along in 1971. Although the cubic-inch displacements may be the same, the 351C and 351W (for Windsor) share almost nothing in design. There are a multitude of differences between these engines, but if you're in doubt as to which you have, look at the fuel pump. The mounting bolts on 351 Windsor fuel pumps are in a line horizontally, like the earlier 289 and 302 engines it was developed from. The newer 351 Cleveland

engine has the bolts in a *vertical* line. Since the Ford factory changed their designations for the Cleveland engines to an "M" suffix (351-M, for instance), identification can sometimes be confusing to the novice.

You'll find that the 335-series engines are generally fitted to the larger cars in the FoMoCo lines, such as the Lincolns, Thunderbirds, LTD's, Cougars and Torinos. Thus, they usually get fitted with all the options, including the air conditioning and power accessories that may make your underhood working room rather limited. Thankfully, the 1975 and later engines that have the most emissions plumbing, also have the solid state

electronic ignition that needs less attention than a points-type system.

Our subject 335-series engine is a 351-M in a 1978 Thunderbird, owned by mechanic Jerry Spotts of Champion Muffler Co., Whittier, California. Jerry has been working on Ford engines for many years and we thought it would be interesting to see how a pro maintains his own engine. Had the vehicle had more mileage, the tune-up might have been in more depth, but further details on the carburetion and solid state ignition can be found in their respective chapters elsewhere in this book. Just remember that a good tune-up man is more than just a parts replacer. ♣

1. The 351C and 400M Ford engines are from the Cleveland engine family and share components. This is a '78 Thunderbird with 351C engine. Arrow is emissions/tuning decal.

2. A proper tuneup begins with a thorough inspection of general engine conditions, such as belt tightness. Inspect for any fluid leaks, battery level, coolant level, or vacuum leaks.

3. As a preventive maintenance check, squeeze all your water hoses; soft and spongy hoses or those showing cracks should be replaced to avoid future cooling system problems.

4. A "quickie" cleanup of the carburetor can be effected by spraying cleaner down the carb with the engine running at a fast idle. This may ruin spark plugs; do it BEFORE changing.

5. This low-mileage Thunderbird needed a few "drivability" changes, so ace mechanic Jerry Spotts of Champion Muffler Co., Whittier, pulls off the Motorcraft 2150 two-barrel carb.

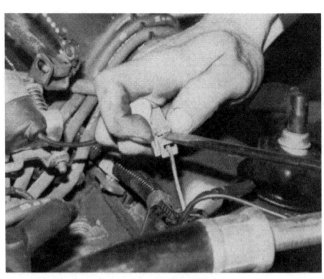

6. A screwdriver must be used carefully to separate the plug for the electric TSP (throttle positioner solenoid) before the carburetor can be lifted clear. Don't break the connector.

7. Just when you think you have everything disconnected and clear, you find there's one more vacuum hose you didn't see! Tag all vacuum lines with masking tape for easy assembly.

8. In the case of this vehicle, the power valve (arrow) was suspect. If yours is bad, the cover will be full of fuel when it is removed. A bad power valve seriously hurts drivability.

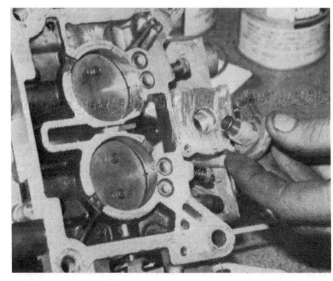

9. Jerry elected to install a new valve with a lower vacuum opening value. The Holley replacement opens at 6.5-in. rather than the stock 10-in. and eliminates flat spots on acceleration.

10. A new cover gasket should come with the new power valve. Make sure when positioning it that the vacuum port (indicated) is not obscured.

11. Jerry's experience with the 2150 led him to also check the accelerator pump condition. The cover comes off with removal of four screws at the front of the carburetor casting.

12. If you're replacing the accelerator pump diaphragm, try to get the older, one-piece model (at left). The current ones with separate shaft can cock in cover after 50,000 miles or so.

13. After the new diaphragm is seated in the carburetor, be sure to reinstall the spring with the LARGE end toward the valve, or the small end will block the valve's operation.

14. Since the carburetor was already off, he decided to re-move the EGR valve for inspection and cleaning. Put rags in intake manifold; clean EGR passages with carbon scraper.

15. The valve can be checked off the engine with a vacuum pump. Start at two inches of vacuum and steadily and slowly increase to 10-in.; EGR valve stem should move smoothly.

16. With new gaskets in place, the carburetor and the EGR spacer and valve are reinstalled. To avoid vacuum leaks, the four bolts should be torqued evenly to 12-15 ft.-lbs.

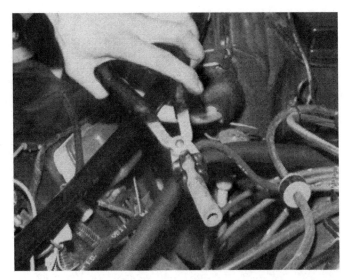

17. Spark plugs should be inspected and cleaned at 10,000 mile intervals, and replaced at 20,000 miles. Use insulated pliers and pull on boots, NOT wires; replacement is $70!

18. A long socket extension and a flex attachment will prove helpful in making plug changes. Gap plugs (.048- to .050-in.), and oil threads lightly (non-gasketed plugs) before installing.

19. High electrical energy is involved in the solid-state Ford ignition, so check the distributor cap, rotor and coil top for signs of cracks, moisture, wear or carbon tracking.

20. Jerry decided to remove the Thunderbird's distributor for a closer examination. Use care with your screwdriver when disconnecting the distributor's electronic ignition connector.

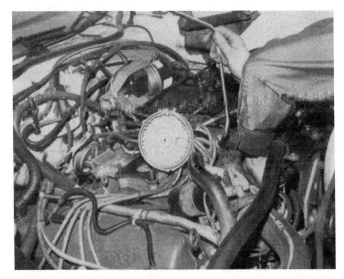

21. A special, angled distributor wrench such as Jerry is holding here is useful in reaching the elusive distributor holddown bolt—buried here behind the air conditioning.

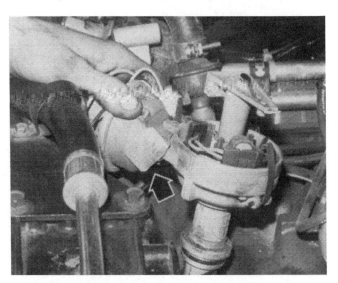

22. Make a chalk mark on the manifold to indicate where the rotor was pointing and pull the distributor out for further work. Identification tag (arrow) is useful in parts ordering.

23. You'll have to consult a Ford manual for the exact specs on the vacuum advance unit, but checking with a vacuum pump will tell you if it's working; watch the plate's movement.

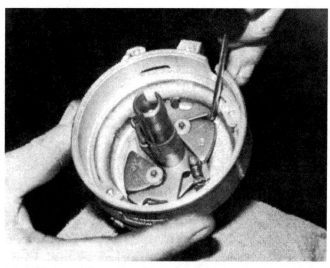

24. With the plate and solid state components removed (see Solid State Ignition chapter), Jerry inspects the weights for the centrifugal advance. These need a dab of cam lubricant.

25. Connections on the solid state coils are exposed with solid brass buttons; wires go on with plastic plug. Jerry routinely cleans off accumulated grime with WD-40 spray.

26. Clogging fuel filters seem to be a problem with some new Fords. Changing one is easy, just cut off the old hose clamps with side-cutter pliers, pull hose and unscrew the filter.

27. Ordinarily, the inline fuel filter is replaced at 20,000 miles, but may clog up earlier depending on the fuel you use. Jerry inspects this one to see if he can see light through it.

28. On all Motorcraft carbs except the 2700 VV, the filter simply screws into the carb body. On the 2700, it is inside the carburetor, behind the fuel line and its inlet fitting.

29. With the engine running again, check the engine at idle for vacuum or fuel leaks at the carburetor, then hook up a timing light and set timing to the specs on your engine decal.

30. The long screw on the TSP solenoid is used for adjustments. On air conditioned cars like this one, it's for "AC-On" speed; on others for anti-dieseling. Adjust as per your decal.

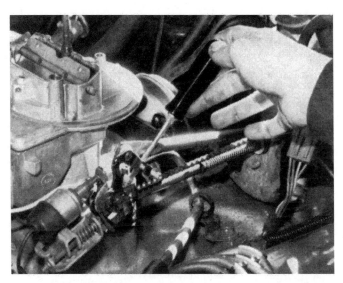

31. "AC-On" adjustment should have been made with AC turned on. Adjust curb idle with AC (and TSP) off, using this screw. Run the engine at high idle for 20 secs., check rpm.

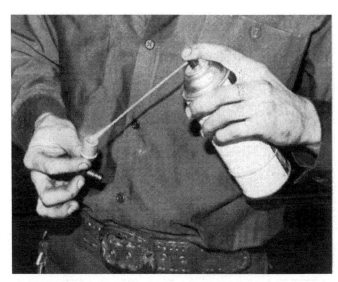

32. Your PCV (Positive Crankcase Ventilation) valve should be cleaned whenever you do preventive maintenance, and replaced whenever you can't hear it rattle if you shake the valve.

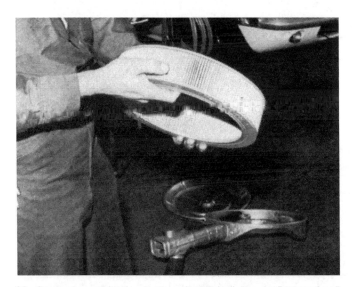

33. Drop your old air cleaner element flatly against a hard floor a few times to shake off dirt, then inspect the pleated paper element. If you can't see a droplight through it, replace.

34. Reinstall the metal portion of the air cleaner on the carb, hooking up the vacuum lines correctly. Wipe the inside clean and clean or replace the PCV filter inside (arrow).

335 FAMILY

351C–351M–400: Race or Torque, They Deliver

351C: NASCAR TECHNIQUE FOR THE STREET

The 351C (Cleveland) is a hybrid engine. The first of the 335 family, it's a cross between a 429 and production small-block technology. Introduced in 1970 and produced until 1974, the 351C was used in Mustangs, Cougars, Torinos and Montegos—no full-size autos or trucks. It was manufactured in both 2-barrel and four-barrel versions with horsepower ratings of 250 at 4600 rpm and 300 at 5400 rpm. Torque output is 355 ft.-lb. at 2600 rpm for the two-barrel and 380 at 3400 rpm for the 4-barrel. Both a Boss and a Cobra Jet version of the 351C were produced in 1971, and a High Output version was made in 1972. The 351C shares many features with the 302 Boss, yet it is dimensionally very different. Because of these differences, very few parts interchange. The same is true for interchanges with the 351W (Windsor) small-block and the two other engines in the 335 family: the 351M and the 400. (Dimensional differences between the 351C and 351M/400 are discussed in the 351M/400 section of this article.)

While the 351C has a cast-in timing chain cover, the 90-degree small-block has a bolt-on snout. The housing incorporates both the water passages and the thermostat pocket. It routes the water from the head through the block and then to the radiator. This design makes for quick, even warm-ups without hot spots, especially around the valves but scuttles any serious interchange. Although the 351C has the same bore spacing, head bolt pattern and thin-wall casting, the crankshaft main and rod journals have different diameters. About the only things that fit both the 351C and other small-blocks are the heads, and these require machining to reroute water passages.

The crankshaft is a nodular cast-iron unit with five mains and six counterweights. Like its small-block siblings, the crank is externally balanced and has 2.75-inch diameter main journals an 2.31-inch rod journals. All early engines used two-bolt main caps. The exceptions are the '71 Boss and CJ versions. After 1971 the four-barrel 351Cs (including the '72 H.O. version) were factory four-bolted, but the two-barrels kept their two-bolt format. The H.O. and Boss cranks were drawn from production stock and Brinell tested to ensure strength.

Modifications to the reciprocating assemblies were also made, and they

Instead of a bolt-on timing cover, a flat steel stamping covers the timing chain and forms the rear of the water pump housing.

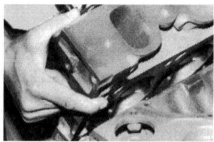

A key difference between the Cleveland and Windsor engines lies in the head-to-block coolant passage. Coolant from the head passes from the square opening of the Cleveland just above the finger and into the block.

The Motorsport forged piston, part No. M-6108-C341, fits the 351M. Fitted on the 76cc head, the compression ratio is about 9:1—just right for today's gasoline.

Motorsport piston, part No. M-6108-B341, fits 351C engines. Ratios are 12:1 on the 351 four-barrel and 12.05:1 on the Boss 351. On two-barrel and '72-'74 four-barrel heads with 76cc chambers, compression is a healthy 10.6:1. Motorsport pistons are also equipped with piston pins.

Next is the M-6108-A401 forged piston for the 400. With its 78cc combustion chamber volume, this piston will generate an 8:1 compression ratio.

vary with engine type. Standard forged steel rods measured 5.780 inches and used ⅜ inch bolts. Boss and H.O. versions use the same forged-steel rods but are fastened with high-strength 180,000-psi yield bolts, which like the crankshafts were specifically tested for strength. Rod end diameters are 2.436 inches and .911-inch, respectively.

Four types of pistons are used in all 351C variants: The two and four-barrel versions use flat-top ('70-'72) and dished ('73-'74) cast aluminum pistons with two valve reliefs. The H.O. used a similar piston but was forged aluminum. The 351 Boss engine uses a forged-aluminum pop-up piston.

Heads on the 351C share the Boss 302 chamber design—a polyangle

wedge that allows the use of canted valves. Canting the valves lets the gases travel in a straighter line than with in-line valve positioning, plus allows larger valve diameter by positioning the valve away from the cylinder walls.

Since several variations of the 351C were built, the heads were modified to optimize the specific engine variant performance. Dimensional changes were made to the combustion chamber (the open type having more cc capacity than the closed type), and valve porting, for each application. Modifications were also done to accept either a hydraulic or mechanical valvetrain. Hence, the two-barrel 351C head has 76.2cc open-type chambers with 2.03-inch intake and 1.66-inch exhaust valve

Motorsport also has the 351C two-barrel cylinder head, part No. M-6049-C351. Intake ports (left) are smaller in volume than 351C four-barrel heads, but the smaller port volume enhances low-rpm gas flow for better street performance. The exhaust ports (right), like the intake side, use the stock bolt pattern.

The slotted pedestals on the Motorsport heads make them ready for nonadjustable hydraulic valvetrains. If you want an adjustable valvetrain, mill the pedestals for screw-in studs.

A 62cc quench-style combustion chamber is used. With flat-top pistons, the compression ratio is 10.5:1. Valves are stock 351C two-barrel, with 2.03-inch intake and 1.65-inch exhaust. These heads are a nice bolt-on 50 horsepower boost for a Windsor or Cleveland block.

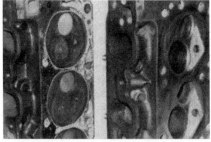

The Boss 302 head (right) and the 351C four-barrel (left) are similar in design. Both have an open-type combustion chamber with a partial quench area for higher compression and turbulence for a better burn. Notice the large oval ports on both heads and the location of the water passages.

SWAP TALK: Here is the difference between adjustable (left) and nonadjustable rockers. If you have nonadjustable-type heads you can modify them to work with a mechanical cam. Making the swap to a mechanical cam on the 351C means using 302 Boss valvetrain components. The rocker arm pedestals have to be machined.

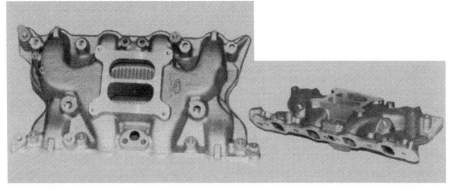

Motorsport also has an intake manifold (part No. M-9424-G351) to fit 351C two-barrel Cleveland heads only. The stock Cleveland four-barrel intake won't fit because the ports don't match (left), and the manifold won't fit on a Windsor application since the intake has no coolant passage (right). In addition, the manifold is too narrow for the 351W block.

head diameters with small (relative to the four barrel heads) oval ports. The four-barrel engine had 62.8cc closed-type chambers in 1070-'71, 75.4cc in 1972 and 1973 and 78.4cc in 1974. All years had 2.19-inch intake and 1.71-inch exhaust valves with larger oval ports. The '71 CJ version used the four-barrel porting and valve sizing with 76.2cc open-type chambers. The Boss version used the four-barrel head but had 66.1cc closed-type chambers, while the H.O. had 75.4cc open-type chambers. Both used adjustable valvetrains since these engines were equipped with mechanical cams.

351M/400: BUILT FOR THE LONG HAUL

The 351M and 400 engines are second in the 335 engine family. The 351M and 400 engines are usually discussed together since the 351M is a destroked version of the 400. The 400 was produced from 1971-'81 and the 351M from 1975-'79, with the "M" used to distinguish the 351M from the 351C. The 400 is used primarily in full-size passenger cars, and although it did make an appearance in a few trucks, the 351M got most of the truck application.

Both these engines are based on the

351C, and though they look almost identical, dimensionally they are quite different. The 351M/400 block has a deck 1.09 inches higher than 351C, and the main journals have different diameters. The 351M/400 has 3-inch journals as opposed to the 2.75-inch 351C journals. The front intake manifold mounting surface is higher on the 351M/400 to allow for both the additional deck height and the cast-in-water bypass metering orifice. The 351M differs from the 400 in that it has a shorter stroke (3.50 versus 4.00 inches) and uses a piston with a higher compression height (1.947 inches versus 1.647 inches).

Pistons for both engines have the same diameter and are cast-aluminum dished units with two valve reliefs. Connecting rods are the same for both engines and have a center-to-center length of 6.580 inches. The big and little ends have respective diameters of 2.435 inches and .973-inch.

Heads for the 351M/400 are very similar to the 351C heads and in fact interchange. The heads have open-type 78.4cc chambers with 2.041-inch intake and 1.654-inch exhaust valve diameters and use the same type of stamped steel rockers as the standard 351C. In 1971 the 400 had a compression ratio of 9.0:1, which was lowered in 1972 to 8.4:1 where it remained until the end of production in 1980. The 351M had a compression ratio of 8.0:1 its entire production run.

On the subject of parts interchange for performance enhancement, little can be said because interchange is very limited—the heads are about the only component that swap. The 302 Boss heads fit the Cleveland-style block if the water passages are rerouted and the proper hardened pushrod and mechanical cam are used. The same consideration should be given to installing Cleveland heads on a 302 Boss. You can make the heads fit, but you'll need to adjust the water passages and compression ratio.

For a bolt-on performance boost to the 351C, 351M and 400, SVO has

351C two-barrel heads, part No. M-6049-C351. Their smaller port volume helps low rpm torque and power, plus 62 cc head chambers produce a 10.5:1 compression ratio with flat top pistons. To complete the package, add SVO's four-barrel intake manifold, part No. M 9424-G351, which matches the head's port size.

Keep in mind when interchanging these components that all the related items must be checked for proper clearance and tolerances. Many good Ford performance specialty shops are around to advise you, and they are as close as your phone or mailbox. A selection of Motorsport distributors is listed in the back of the book. ∎

Overall Engine Dimensions

The dimensions given are for an average engine of the make and size listed, but remember that intake and exhaust manifold variations on the same engine in different years may result in slight differences. Similarly, the dimensions given are overall measurements, including such things as air cleaners, oil filters, water pump fan, etc., but not bellhousings. Engines using the serpentine belt drive system, of course, would be slightly shorter.

Engine Family	Displacement	Wi	Ln	Ht	Wt
335-Series (Cleveland)	351C-Boss 351	25½	29	29	550
	351M-400	26	29	29	575

Critical Bolt Torques (ft.-lbs.)

	351C- M -400
Bolt-Cylinder Head Step 1 Step 2 Step 3	55 65 95-100
Bolt-Intake Manifold	23-25 28-32
Bolt-Connecting Rod	40-45
Bolt-Main Bearing Caps	95-105-Inner/Two Bolt 35-45-Outer
Stud-Rocker Arm Bolt-Rocker Arm	65-75 17-23 351C Hydraulic Cam

If the large oval ports don't catch your eye, a 351C four-barrel head can also be identified by the numeral 4 cast in the corner.

The 351C two-barrel open-combustion chamber heads are identified by their lack of quench area, increasing the volume of the head and reducing the compression ratio. Later production four-barrel heads also have the open-style combustion chambers but have larger intake and exhaust ports.

The difference in port size between four-barrel Cleveland heads (top) and two-barrel (bottom) is dramatic and easily seen.

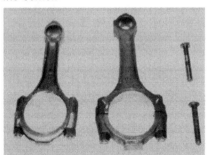

The 351C Boss rod (left) can be distinguished from the regular production 351C rod (right) by use of 180,000-psi yield, ⅜-inch interference-fit bolts on spot-faced bolt seats.

The 351C two-barrel heads can also be identified by the numeral 2 cast in one corner on the top of the head.

The 351M/400 block is distinguished from the 351C block by its increased deck height and accompanying extra material around the distributor hole, as well as its larger main bearing journals.

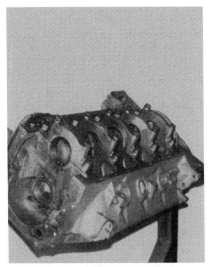

The 351C came with four-bolt mains in Boss, H.O., CJ and four-barrel versions produced in 1972 and 1973.

You can recognize a 351C block by the cast-in timing chain housing. This snout also contains water passages, thermostat and coolant-metering orifice.

In 1971, 1972 and 1973, 351C four-barrel engines came equipped with this type of cast-iron spread bore manifold.

The engine should never be operated without this by-pass orifice in place, even if no thermostat is used. Otherwise the majority of the coolant will flow directly into the water pump rather than to the radiator, causing overheating.

The two types of 351C valve stems are shown here. The single groove is used with mechanical cams and produces a tight grip, inhibiting rotation. The multi-grooved valve stem is used wth hydraulic cams and promotes valve rotation.

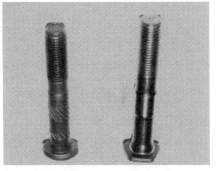

The rod cap bolt on the right is the 180,000-psi yield 351C Boss interference bolt. On the left is the production knurled Cleveland rod cap bolt.

Blue Print Dimensions	351C	351 Boss/ H.O.	351M	400
Deck Clearance	.035	.035	.0565	.0565
Main Bearing Clearance	.0011 - .0028			
Rod Bearing Clearance	.0008 - .0026			
Cam Shaft Bearing Clearance	.001 - .003			
Crankshaft End Play	.004 - .010			
Con Rod (2 rods) Side Clearance	.010 - .020			
Valve stem to guide - Exhaust	.0015 - .0032			
- Intake	.0010 - .0027			
Valve Lash	Hydraulic	.026 - .028 hot	Hydraulic	Hydraulic
Piston to Valve Clearance	.070 - Intake/ .100 Exhaust MIN.			
Piston to Bore	.0034 - .0042			
Piston to Pin	.0006 - .0008			
Piston pin to con rod	interference			
Piston ring gap (No. 1 comp.)	.010 - .020			
(No. 2 comp.)	.010 - .020			
(Oil ring)	.015 - .055			
Firing Order	1-3-7-2-6-5-4-8			

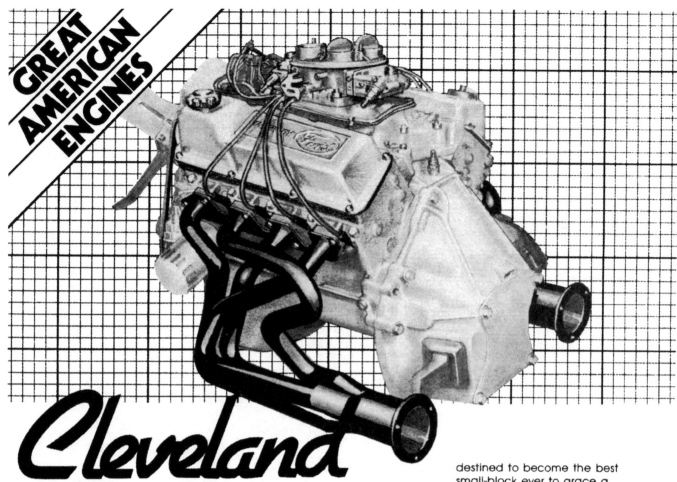

Cleveland Ford

By Jeff Smith

Boss, hip, groovy, far out and heavy—remember them? They were the hip generation's slang of the late Sixties. Ford jumped on the youth-oriented roller coaster ride of musclecars and finally found a winner in the small-block Cleveland engines. Light powerplants with excellent power capabilities due to their big-port heads, the Cleveland

The Boss of Ford Performance

engines trace their heritage back to the Trans Am courses and the vaunted Tunnel Port engines.

The rumors that the Tunnel Port engines would become production items were rampant during late 1968 and early '69. But it was not

to be. Instead came the Boss 302 as the street version of the Tunnel Port, with canted valves and all the makings of a very strong street engine. The Boss motor arrived at a crucial time for Ford, because it filled the void created by the missing high-performance 289 that was dropped in 1968. Although Ford did have the 4-barrel 302 in 1968, it was not a performance engine. But the Boss was a different story. Rated at 290hp at 5800 rpm, the big bore/short stroke motor was a natural high-winder. The efficient canted valve head design that accommodated large valves, the four-bolt main block, forged steel cross-drilled crank (the only forged crank to come in any Cleveland engine), and aluminum intake manifold with a 780 cfm Holley were race-bred pieces that left little doubt about Ford's performance stance. The first heads for the Boss 302 came out with 2.23-inch intake valves and 57cc combustion chambers. By 1970, however, the valve size had been reduced to 2.19 inches to help the bottom end torque slightly by increasing intake charge velocity.

The Boss 302 also formed the basis for a new Ford engine,

destined to become the best small-block ever to grace a Dearborn engine compartment. The beginning of the new decade in 1970 saw the introduction of the 351 Cleveland. Named after the Ohio plant where the engines were

Mouse Trap

Although building a better mousetrap will never have the world knocking on Jeff Grueninger's Columbia, Illinois door, it's bound to frighten more than one rodent-powered street cruiser. It's not that Jeff's 1972 Gran Torino Sport is especially frightening to look at—its pearl white base paint is brightened with a candy-colored stripe and Fenton spokers with a combination of Formula and Douglas tires. Applying the gear multiplication is a merger of a Trans-Go assisted FMX tranny and a Ford 9-inch differential carrying 4.88 gears.

But the bait for the trap is a 351 Cleveland motor with '71 closed chambered heads and a Sig Erson cam, lifters and rocker arms. The rest of the engine is basically stock except for the Thorley headers, Offenhauser manifold, Mallory ignition and a little steel braided sparkle by Competition Plumbing of St. Louis. Jeff's own fender flares and a blue velvet interior finish the Torino's show quality appearance. But don't let it fool you; it's still a baited trap for any unsuspecting mouse.

built (which differentiated the new engine from the Windsor Ford built in Canada), the 351C utilized the canted valve arrangement first used by Ford in the Boss 302.

The Cleveland motors were produced in two configurations initially: a 2-barrel model with open chambered heads for reduced emissions, and a 4-barrel model that used wedge or quench-type chambers. The 4-barrel engines also had larger valves and ports, and a slightly hotter hydraulic cam to handle the better breathing. The higher horsepower 351C was rated at 300hp with an honest 11.0:1 compression ratio.

These two engines were also offered the following year, but it was the introduction of the Boss 351 in '71 that had all the Ford fanatics talking. The Boss 351 came with four-bolt mains, a high nodular iron content crankshaft, forged 11.3:1 pistons and a good mechanical cam that necessitated the use of the '71 4-barrel heads with milled rocker stands required for the adjustable rocker arms.

Yearly Beloved...

CID	Bore & Stroke	1969	70	71	72	73	74	75	76	77	78	79
BOSS 302	(4.00 x 3.00)	■■■■■										
351C	(4.00 x 3.50)	■■■■■■■■■■									
BOSS 351	(4.00 x 3.50)			■								
351 H.O.	(4.00 x 3.50)		■■■■■								
351CJ	(4.00 x 3.50)			■■■■■■							
400	(4.00 x 4.00)		■■■■■■■■■■■■■■■■■■						

The unique feature of the Cleveland engine is the canted arrangement of the valves which benefits the breathing characteristics of the engine by providing smoother transitions for both intake and exhaust gases. This close-up reveals the slot used for the nonadjustable hydraulic lifter engines.

Breathin' Easy

GREAT AMERICAN ENGINES

Pick a Number

Ford

C9ZZ-6564-A ...Boss 302-351C adjustable rocker arm
C9ZZ-6A528-A ...Boss 302-351C sled type rocker fulcrum
C9ZZ-6A527-A ...Boss 302-351C thread-in rocker arm stud
C50Z-12127-E ...Boss 302 dual-point mechanical advance distributor

Tubular Automotive

ES7 ....351C headers; 1960-'66 Mustang, Comet, Falcon and 1970-'76 Maverick, Comet
ES17 ....Boss 302 headers; 1960-'66 Mustang, Comet, Falcon and 1970-'76 Maverick, Comet

TRW

50048 ....Boss 302 high-volume oil pump
L2324F ....Boss 302 10.5 compression piston
CB948P ....Boss 302 rod bearings with 3/16-inch dowel hole
MS2975P ....Boss 302 main bearings with full oil groove
50086 ....351C high-volume oil pump
CB962P ....351C rod bearings with 3/16-inch dowel hole
MS3010P ....351C main bearings with full oil groove

Manley

43540 ....Boss 302-351C adjustable rocker arms
42103 ....Boss 302-351C rocker arm stud
42156 ....Boss 302-351C push rod guide plate
25752 ....Boss 351C push rod
25728 ....Boss 302 push rod
25750 ....351C (not 351 Boss push rod)
41860 ....351C rocker stud boss cutter
43305 ....Boss 302-351C aluminum needle bearing rocker arm with 7/16-inch rocker stud

Boss Bomb

lthough the Boss 302 was the first Ford canted valve engine in production, the 1971 Boss 351 became the most powerful. Limited numbers of the Boss 351 Mustangs were produced. The selection of factory performance parts is slim, but the aftermarket industry still stocks many of the items to make the Boss a serious challenger on the street.

Pony Oats

Mating the 351C to any early Mustang or Falcon body has always been a popular swap among Ford streeters looking for a rapid ride in an inconspicuous vehicle. The clearance between the shock towers is tight, but the engine will fit, although the changeover can be called anything but a mere bolt-in. Headers available from Tubular Automotive (248 Weymouth St., Rockland, MA 02370) will make the swap more convenient, since their ES7 model headers are designed for the 1960-'66 Comet, Mustang and Falcon and the 1970-'76 Maverick and Comet.

This swap also necessitates converting the oil filter mount to an Econoline right-angle adapter (Ford PN C5TZ-6881-A and bolt PN C5TZ-6894-A), along with small-block motor mounts to mate the engine to the chassis. A Boss 351 or 351CJ motor would certainly elevate the lowly Falcon into the limelight, especially if the package were adequately disguised as a bone-stock boulevardier.

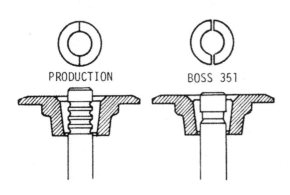

PRODUCTION   BOSS 351

Squeeze Play

Production Cleveland engines came with three-tiered valve locks that allowed the valve to rotate in the keeper, thus promoting longer valve life. Boss 351s use a single groove to lock the valve against the retainer. Moderate rpm street engines can benefit from using the stock production keepers and retainers; single grooves are recommended if extreme rpm racing is in the engine's future.

98

Drip Tip

A no-cost way to keep your Cleveland engine from fouling your clean garage floor is to offset the rear main seal when assembling the engine. Instead of aligning the seal flush with the parting surfaces of the main bearing caps, allow the seal to protrude about ⅛-inch on one side. This will prevent oil seepage between the seal faces. In addition, 1971-'73 351 CJ four-bolt main blocks use a pin to locate the standard rope seal. When replacing this rope seal with a neoprene seal, drive the pin out of the main bearing cap and fill the hole with silicone. If the pin is not removed, seal damage and possible engine seizure may result.

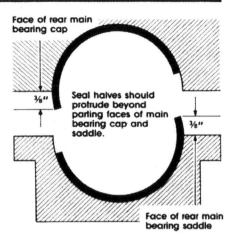

Face of rear main bearing cap

Seal halves should protrude beyond parting faces of main bearing cap and saddle.

⅛" ⅛"

Face of rear main bearing saddle

Pedestal Power

Stock 351C 4-barrel heads used with a hydraulic camshaft can be converted to the Boss style heads by milling the slotted rocker pedestals .300-inch to allow clearance for the adjustable rocker arms. Care must be taken to mill the pedestals parallel to the bottom of the original slot, and not parallel to the bottom of the head.

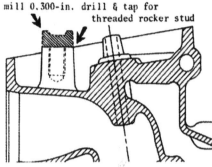

mill 0.300-in. drill & tap for threaded rocker stud

The slot is at a compound angle that is required for the canted valve arrangement. After milling the pedestal, the stud hole must be drilled out with a .372-inch bit and tapped with a 7/16-14 NC bottoming tap for the screw-in stud.

The sled-type fulcrums on the stock Ford system keep the rocker arms in place, but are prone to breakage. If you are running a guide plate with hardened push rods (these are necessary for solid lifters anyway), using big-block Chevy rockers and ball fulcrums will reduce your breakage problem considerably. That is, of course, if you can bring yourself to put Chevy parts in your Dearborn motor.

Spare the Rod

Boss 351 connecting rods are machined from SAE 1041 steel and are shotpeened and Magnafluxed to insure durability. Rod bolts of 180,000 psi are used, and are capable of high rpm use. This rod has been machined to accept full floating pins. The connecting rods used in the low-performance 2-barrel engines can also be used for limited street action if reinforced with high tensile strength bolts (like the SPS bolts) and the casting flash is removed to prevent stress concentrations.

Boss I.D.

A quick way to identify a Boss 302 block is to look at the freeze plugs. The Boss 302 used special screw-in freeze plugs, while the more pedestrian 302 engines used common press-in freeze plugs. Boss 302 blocks also had four-bolt main caps and came with forged steel cranks. Early forged cranks came from the factory cross-drilled.

Oil Fall Down

One of the weak points in the Cleveland engines is in the lubrication system. Extreme oil pressure is required to prevent oil starvation at the rod bearings. This is due to the unique way the oil passages are designed. Oil from the filter is routed across the number one main cap and cam bearings to the large gallery on the engine's right side. Passages from this gallery direct the oil to the main and rod bearings, and then to the cam bearings. One way to decrease the tendency toward marginal rod bearing lubrication is to install restrictor plugs (such as Moroso's kit, PN 2205) in the main

bearing saddles. This limits the amount of oil that reaches the cam bearings and diverts it to the main bearings. Additional lubrication

can be afforded the main bearings by using full groove bearings such as TRW's MS 3010P and a high-volume oil pump.

GREAT AMERICAN ENGINES
Cleveland Ford

In addition, the Boss 351 featured a different intake manifold and carburetor. Previous Clevelands had used the standard flange 4300-A Holley/Motorcraft carburetor. But the Boss engine, and the subsequent Cobra Jet 351 engine that debuted in May, 1971, used a spreadbore model 4300-D Motorcraft carburetor. The 351CJ that came out in mid-year combined parts from both the 4-barrel engine and the Boss 351 to produce a performance choice for the enthusiast. Although not as radical as the Boss engine, the 351CJ utilized the same four-bolt main block but used low-compression open chamber heads and rocker pedestals designed for a hydraulic camshaft that had slightly longer duration and more lift than the stock 4-barrel cam.

In addition to the 351CJ engine, Ford also introduced a larger version of the Cleveland engine with 400 cubic inches. Only offered as a 2-barrel engine from 1971-'79, the engine never received much notice from the Dearborn hot rodders and was relegated to the lowly status of powering Ford's larger cars. The 400 used a crankshaft with a ½-inch longer stroke to come up with its "square" specs—but unfortunately, this item cannot be used in the 351C engines as a stroker crank because of its larger main bearing journals. The 400 block is 1 inch taller than the 351C to accommodate the longer stroke, which limits intake manifold selection to just the ones designed specifically for the 400.

The year 1972 signaled the beginning of the end for the high-compression Cleveland engines. The Boss 351 survived for one more year as the 351 H.O. (or High Output), although compression dropped to 9.2:1 with the installation of open chambered heads. The mechanical cam was also revamped and given slightly less duration and a little more lift. The Cobra Jet motor survived and was tagged as the 351C 4-barrel for part of 1972. The engine specs remained intact except for a four-degree cam retard in the valve specifications.

The following year dropped the final curtain for the short-lived 351C. Compression fell to 8.0:1 in all the 351's, and the H.O. engine disappeared from the option list. The only "performance" engine available that year in the Cleveland format was the 351CJ that made its final appearance as a 266hp model with dished pistons and a hydraulic cam.

After the Cleveland engines vanished, the demand for the 351W engines was such that in 1975 Ford introduced a little-known engine designated the 351M or "modified." This engine was a crossbreed between the 400 block and the 351W crankshaft, which gave 351 cubic inches with a tall deck height. It was only offered with a 2-barrel.

Unquestionably, the Cleveland engines, especially the Boss 351, were the best small-blocks that Ford ever produced. It's unfortunate that the engine came out at the onset of the smog-engine era. Due to low production numbers, Ford never produced a large number of performance parts, and many of the ones still available are difficult to locate.

But even with their limited availability, the 351 Clevelands show a tremendous amount of promise as good street performers. The canted-valve head design is responsive in street trim and has proved to be a definite contender even in the twilight zone of Pro Stock racing. Cleveland, Ohio, may never enjoy the romantic associations of other great cities, but it will always be a favorite with Ford horsepower devotees.

Printed in Great Britain
by Amazon

44474765R00057